ANGLESEY PAST AND PRESENT

Anglesey
Past and Present

Wendy Hughes

GWASG Carreg Gwalch

ISBN: 0-86381-560-X

Cover design: Alan Jones

First published in 1999 by
Gwasg Carreg Gwalch, 12 Iard yr Orsaf, Llanrwst, Wales LL26 0EH
℡ 01492 642031   ▤ 01492 641502
✆ books@carreg-gwalch.co.uk   Website: www.carreg-gwalch.co.uk

CONTENTS

INTRODUCTION

Anyone wishing for a tranquil 'close-to-nature' holiday must visit the Isle of Anglesey (Ynys Môn). The tourist guides describe it as the Land of Inspiration, and anyone seeking to return home with fortified strength and memorable impressions will not be disappointed.

Here you will find, unfurling like a banner, a golden pageant of history. Every period is represented and, as evidence of early man and the cromlech builders intermingle with the Iron Age hill-forts, visitors are left wondering how such magnificent monuments could have been erected in a time when mechanical equipment was yet to be invented.

The now cleared sacred oak groves, once home to the singing Druids, leave us thinking of an island that was once the centre for Druidism, a culture and religion that is still a mystery, and still widely misunderstood. As long as the Druid religion flourished, the Roman Empire knew that its political future was uncertain in these islands. To overcome that uncertainty, an Army was sent to Môn to destroy the communities and slaughter the unarmed Druids. The Romans destroyed the centre of Druidism, and left behind some Latin words as well as Christianity, their recently adopted faith.

Next came the 'Age of the Saints' and their period is represented in such places as Penmon Priory and St Seiriol's well. In turn the Danes, who came in search of new lands, returned empty-handed but took Christianity with them. Next came the rulers of Gwynedd who set up their palace at Aberffraw, from where they dominated the whole of Wales. When the English invaded and put an end to Welsh independence in the 13th century, Edward I was prompted to build a spectacular series of castles, one of which was built in Beaumaris, and still stands proud within the medieval town. Penmynydd has a history of its own and is remembered as the home of the Tudur family who later ruled from the English throne.

Industrial history is represented by farming and fishing, and a visit to the working windmill at Llynon is an experience not to be missed. The old quarries and copper workings left by a once thriving industry are represented in the ravaged Mynydd Parys, where the mind of the visitor will be fired with vivid pictures of industrial activity.

Equally as impressive are the engineering skills used to build the two bridges that link the island to the mainland. Telford's bridge was the world's first big iron suspension bridge, whilst the smaller tubular Britannia bridge carried the first London to Holyhead express train in 1850.

The island has some of the most varied coastline in Britain. Here the visitor can meander along 200 kilometres of golden beaches, or join one of the many guided tours arranged by the Coastal Heritage Centre at Llys Llywelyn. Anglesey offers a wealth of natural beauty, flora and fauna. It also has many contemporary attractions to suit every age and interest. These range from the butterfly and bird palace to exploring the world of nuclear energy at Wylfa power station. Or perhaps you would prefer to visit the underwater world at Anglesey's Sea Zoo where you can observe five hundred fish, shipwrecks and a lobster farm. At Parc Henblas dad can enjoy a leisurely game of golf, whilst mum can browse through the many craft centres and the children enjoy a fun day at Adventureland. You can board the Island Princess and take a cruise to Puffin island from Beaumaris, or maybe visit Ireland from the port of Holyhead.

The Welsh name for Anglesey is Môn. From around the 12th century it has also sometimes been called 'Môn, Mam Cymru' (Anglesey, mother of Wales). One claim states that this derives from the fact that the inhabitants of the less productive mountainous regions of North Wales flourished, thanks to the grain supplied from the ample Môn cornfields. Later, when Welsh resistance fighters were encamped in the Snowdonia mountains, Edward I called on the English navy to help prevent the traffic of grain between the island and the mainland.

A second possible reason for the reference to motherhood in the name Môn has its roots in Celtic paganism, when the Druids worshipped the goddess of fertility.

Some authorities believe that the Norse name, Anglesey, derives from Ôndull's Eye, after a Viking chieftain who invaded sometime during the period 850 to 1050 when the island became embroiled in two hundred years of fierce Norse raids. Or perhaps the Saxon King Egbert, who invaded the island in 853, named it Angle's Ey (Isle of the Angles)?

Môn, like any good mother, has always provided for her inhabitants. The rich soil allows for excellent farming, and the lush green pastures have enabled farm animals to be reared in large numbers for many centuries. The coastal villages once thrived from seafaring and fishing and at one time the natural minerals of copper and lead ore, provided Anglesey with an important source of wealth. Today tourism has replaced most of these redundant industries.

On the whole the island is lightly populated, with just five main market towns. Outside these, the inhabitants live in hamlets, many have white-washed cottages and winding lanes, providing the holiday-maker with an ideal setting in which to relax and explore.

Although small, Môn is a progressive island and can claim to be the first in many areas. In 1915, at the suggestion of a Canadian visitor, the first meeting of the Women's Institute held in Britain took place in Llanfairpwllgwyngyllgogerychwyrndrobwllllantysiliogogogoch – the village with the longest name. It means 'St Mary's Church in the hollow of the white hazel near a rapid whirlpool and the Church of St Tysilio near the red cave.' The village name expanded from the original Llanfair Pwllgwyngyll sometime in the last century, in an attempt to develop the village as a commercial and tourist centre. It is believed that a committee was formed to find ways to encourage trains and 19th century tourists to stop at the village; and an enterprising cobbler from Menai Bridge came up with the name. Little did he know that he had inadvertently thought of one of the most successful tourist marketing plans of all time! Although the train station is no more, tourists still flock to see the signpost, and to purchase a souvenir platform ticket from the local shops.

The first comprehensive school in Wales was opened in Môn in September 1949, and the village of Gwalchmai holds the honour of being the first on the island to have electricity, thanks to a local water-mill! In 1972 Môn was the first area in Wales to have a fluoridated water supply and, in the same year, the second nuclear power station in Wales came into service at Wylfa.

The island is also known for the wide variety of festivals and side-shows which are held throughout the year. Beaumaris Festival is held during the Spring Bank Holiday. Sioe Sir Fôn, or Primin Môn (the Anglesey Agricultural Show) is the largest such event in North Wales and allows the visitor to gain some first hand knowledge of aspects of life on the island. The Menai Bridge Fair, a three hundred year old tradition, takes place on 24 October each year, and offers the out of season visitor a chance to mingle with fortune tellers, participate in the funfair rides, or sample the roasting chestnuts. To commemorate the seven hundredth anniversary of the granting of Anglesey's Royal Charter, numerous extra events were held throughout 1996.

The fabric of Môn is available only to those who take the time to investigate it; before we explore more of this delightful corner of Wales, perhaps we should turn back the clock and take a brief look into the island's fascinating and troubled past.

CHAPTER ONE

THE BIRTH OF THE ISLAND

Ynys Môn is the largest island in the British Isles and has an unique character. The whole island is low-lying, particularly in the south west, and within its two hundred and ninety square miles there are only nine points that reach above one hundred and fifty-two metres. The highest of these summits is Mynydd Caergybi (Holyhead Mountain), which rises in the east of the island to an impressive two hundred and nineteen metres, casting its protective shadow over the rest of the island.

However, Môn hasn't always been an island, and to begin our story we need to go back five hundred thousand years, to a time when it was always winter in Britain. Longer periods of much colder and drier conditions alternated with periods when the climate was much hotter than anything we know today – almost equatorial weather. At this time Môn was part of the low-lying coastal plain of Britain; the Menai Straits and the bays of Caernarfon and Cardigan (Aberteifi) were dry lands. The island, like the majority of Britain, was largely unoccupied, except for the occasional adventurous group of opportunist hunters who braved the elements in pursuit of the seasonal migration of herds, such as mammoth, reindeer, wild horse, bison, and even elephant. For much of the time, Britain was simply a peninsula of mainland Europe, so these groups of people could roam far and wide as they pursued these animals. These early visitors to Britain, were a primitive species of man known as Homo erectus, and the only tools and weapons they used were of stone or flint.

By about one hundred thousand years ago Homo erectus had been superseded by Neanderthal man who sometimes lived in caves, but most often in temporary shelters erected near rivers and lakes. Unearthed skeletons show that Neanderthal man was more robust and muscular than modern man. Tool-making had changed too and the method favoured most by these people is called the Mousterian method after roofs found in a cave by Le Moustier in the Dordogne region of France. Unlike the earlier tools, which were made from shaped stone these tools were made from stone flakes, each struck from the stone 'core', which had been trimmed in advance. Neanderthal man never grasped the potential of bone as a material for tools, or the art of sewing. However they would have needed clothing to keep warm in the cold spells. Garments were fashioned by using animal's skins and stone tools. First the hide would have been laid flat and, with the aid of a stone scraper, all the bits of flesh and fat removed. After the skin had been dried it would have been cured in the smoke of a smouldering fire to toughen it and seal the pores. The pieces for the garment would have been cut with a stone knife and holes punched along the edges of the skins with a pointed stone. The pieces were then placed on the wearer and laced together with narrow strips of rawhide – like a sort of skin toga. Shoes were also made in the same way.

By the time the last glaciers engulfed Britain Neanderthal man had been succeeded by Homo sapiens – the people who are genetically identical to man today. Any evidence of these early Palaeolithic or Old Stone Age encampments would have been swept away by the re-appearance of the glaciers during the last Ice Age. The only information we have is that deduced from studying the remains excavated from caves and shelters that were occupied at the onset of the last glaciation. Several of these sites have been located in North Wales, particularly around the limestone headlands of the Great and Little Ormes and at Kendrick's cave in Llandudno, where some of the earliest artefacts have been found. These are a set of decorated deer teeth and an unusual horse jaw, carved with sharply cut zigzag patterns. Although their authenticity has been doubted, most agree that they date from about 30,000 BC, or just before the severe climate that drove people from the region for some 15,000 years.

During the last glaciation Britain was deserted, but after the ice retreated around 12,000 BC, humans returned. The warmer weather brought an increase in thick woodland, which became the home of a variety of animals still familiar to us today. Hunting animals and gathering fruits and plants remained the way of life for these tribal communities who travelled over vast areas in search of food. By studying the remains of butchered animals from this period, scientists have been able to tell us a great deal about the lifestyle of early man. Many of the foot bones of horses and red deer found have cut marks on the underside of their toe bones. It has been suggested that this is because the long tendons were extracted by carefully cutting up the feet. These long flexible treads, or tendons, would have been used in many ways – as sewing thread for hides to make clothing, or for binding a spearhead to a shaft. Tool making had become more sophisticated, and included objects made of bone and antler as well as stone. Throwing spears were also used extensively. Artefacts from this period are usually known as tools from the Creswellian period, after the first items found in the Creswell Crags on the borders of Derbyshire and Nottinghamshire. These people were also the first to produce cave art and to make art objects, which included animal and human figures of bone and ivory.

With the increase in temperature, the ice-sheets that had once blanketed so much of Britain began to melt. Huge regions of land became flooded, and remnants of the drowned forests may still be seen today at several points along the coast of Anglesey. Although half covered by sand and gravel, the observant visitor can meander between the ancient stumps and roots of the forest trees, and inspect the bones of wild animals that once roamed the land.

The people who occupied Anglesey by 10,000 BC were known as the Mesolithic or Middle Stone Age peoples. They formed small hunting communities, probably made up of immediate family groups. These small mobile groups of hunters, still dependent on wild foods, moved between inland and coastal camps as they took advantage of seasonal foods. The animals they hunted would have been skinned and cooked over small camp-fires and, as in many contemporary hunting societies, we can only surmise that the meat would have been equally shared amongst the clan to dispel any ideas of hierarchical status. As time progressed, they learned to supplement their diet by fishing and gathering shellfish, fruits and nuts. Their lives were simple and not hampered by ideas of fine possessions, social stability or the scarcity of food, which may well have accounted for the increase in population.

They also took full advantage of bone and antlers to make pins, harpoons and needles. They also learned the art of sewing, but how our ancestors perforated the eye of the needle we do not know! One theory is that a crude pointed boring tool was used in much the same way that we use a gimlet today. Another guess is that perhaps a primitive type of rotary drill had been developed. These bone needles, together with the sinews of the animals, were used to join pieces of skin to make into a variety of garments.

The landscape across the whole of Britain underwent a radical change too. By about 10,000 BC the land had changed from open wild tundra to closed woodland dominated by pine and birch. At the end of the ice-ages large blocks of ice flowed from the Irish Sea across Anglesey peeling off the top layer of topsoil or boulder clay. This resulted in a thick layer of very fertile soil being exposed, which determined Anglesey's future character as rich farming country. Today few trees remain on Anglesey, but in those days the centre of the island was densely forested with oak and hazel trees.

Between 8,000 and 6,000 BC, rising sea levels severed the land bridge linking Britain with Europe. Britain became an island and from then on began to develop its own traditions. Eventually, valleys too became flooded, and one of these formed what we now know as the Menai Straits, cutting off Môn from the rest of Britain. Thus Ynys Môn was formed. A rise of thirty metres in the water level made a strait between Traeth Coch (Red Wharf Bay) in the east, and Malltraeth in the south-west, which ultimately created the shape of the island as we see it today. The whole island is made of pre-Cambrian rock on which deposits of shale and limestone are still prominent, especially around the headland at Penmon.

Man finally settled on the island, and one of the early Stone Age camps has been located at Trwyn Du near Aberffraw on the south-western coast of Môn. To visit the site it is best to park at Aberffraw and walk about one kilometre along the river, which is easier at low tide. Today Trwyn Du projects across the estuary of Afon Ffraw but in those days, as the sea level was much lower, it would have looked out over a river valley. Charcoal particles taken from a camp fire dates the site around 7,000 BC, and excavations in 1974 revealed the remnants of tool manufacture as well as a fine scattering of waste flint. These are probably from the sharpened points of their microliths, fine arrow tips used as the dart of their harpoons and fish-spears. Armed with these microliths stone-age man would have hunted down the abundance of red deer that roamed through the woodland. No evidence of firm building structures has been discovered and, although little remains, anyone visiting the site can close their eyes and imagine an everyday stone-age scenario. A small group of women and children eagerly await the return of their menfolk from a hunting expedition, and as they come into sight, a loud cheer is echoed throughout the valley. Tired and hungry the men show-off their bounty, which is then skinned and the meat roasted. It is also possible that ritual chanting and dancing may have taken place around the camp-fire, including the re-enactment of the hunting and final killing. After a good meal is shared by all, the women and children retire to their flimsy skin tents and, as the embers of the fire flicker and fade, the men gather around the camp-fire to tell tales of adventure and bravado. These tales, along with those handed down from their ancestors would have been elaborated to excite and enthral. In this way the traditions of story-telling were passed down to future generations of the clan.

Recent building work carried out in the village of Aberffraw revealed that a number of similar hunting camps had been established along the river banks during the period around 7,000 BC.

CHAPTER TWO

THE BEGINNING OF CIVILIZATION

By 5,000 BC the island of Môn had become more hospitable. The weather continued to slowly improve and a richer, more varied, plant life began to flourish. By now animals more comfortable with the colder climate, like reindeer, had disappeared and man was left to use the land, and its natural resources, as best he could.

The most significant event in history took place between 4,400 and 3,800 BC when farming was first adopted. Around this time small bands of people from Spain and Portugal, the countries bordering the Mediterranean Sea and Iberian Peninsula, migrated across Europe. Those who settled in Môn probably arrived in dug-out wooden canoes. The idea of using plants and animals to provide a more predictable food supply undoubtedly began with these Iberian people. Whether it was the result of them settling in Britain or the native hunter-gatherer copying ideas from their continental neighbours is impossible to say.

Historians often talk of a sudden leap from a hunting to a farming community, but the archaeological evidence suggests that it was a gradual process of economic and social change. It has also been suggested that this change from a Mesolithic to Neolithic Age was due to a sudden influx of invading warriors, but the change could have been brought about by an invasion of ideas from other lands, rather than of people.

These early farming communities who were looking for new lands in which to plant their grains, a primitive form of wheat or barley, had a considerable impact on the countryside. The oak and hazel trees that had given the early settlers ideal protection from the climate and invading warriors were no longer needed. The dense forests needed to be cleared, and man soon learned that he could do the work quicker by attaching a wooden handle to his stone axe. Botanical research dates the clearing of these woodlands to about 4,000 BC. The rocks of Wales were a useful source of raw material for the making of axes, and although there is no evidence of any axe making factories in Môn, we do know that a large factory did exist at y Graig Lwyd on Mynydd Penmaenmawr, east of Bangor. Excavations have revealed that there was much activity on this site from about 4.000 BC. Penmaenmawr polished stone axes have been found in many parts of Britain and their wide distribution suggests that these people not only had the skill to make quality axes, but also had the ability to organise trade on a large scale. Bangor Museum has a map showing the distribution of the products made at Graig Lwyd, as well as a display showing the various stages of axe manufacture.

In order to harvest the grain that they had planted special tools had to be developed. Excavations have uncovered ingenious sickles that were made by setting short lengths of flint into either suitable handles, or into the sockets of teeth removed from the lower jawbone of animals.

A primitive form of mill has also been discovered which was possibly an adaptation of the mortars used by man during the Ice Age to grind the various pigments used for their cave murals and body art. These mills consisted of a flat piece of sandstone on which the grain was placed and then crushed by using an elongated pebble.

The major change in food-supply bound man to one place for at least as long as the crops took to ripen. This changed the way of life from a predominantly hunting and surviving community to a more settled farming one – the dawn of civilisation and community life as we know it today. Settlements probably comprised of one or two wooden houses usually enclosed, with a causeway entrance.

With the introduction of agriculture, cattle, pigs and, to a lesser degree, sheep and goats were brought possibly from Spain and Portugal. The well drained, easily cultivated rich soil of Môn would have attracted many settlers, especially around the river valleys. The uplands were used mainly for hunting and as a rich source of fine stone used in the manufacture of their tools and weapons. Men became expert farmers and learned to domesticate animals rather than hunt them. The women learned to make rope from horse hair and they also mastered the craft of weaving cloth from the wool of sheep. We do not know when textiles were first made but we know that spun thread was being manufactured because spindle whorls, the small flywheel that fits over the end of the spindle used during the making of thread, have been found at a number of sites. As a community they now had an alternative to the leather garments worn by previous settlers. They also made pottery, and placed wooden handles on their flint weapons, but as yet, they knew nothing about metals.

More spectacular than their arrival were the large megalithic burial monuments in which they buried their dead. At first these were small stone structures, such as portal dolmens and simple passage graves. Very much larger monuments, now called long barrows, or gallery passage graves with a rounded or polygonal chamber followed these. Over the years the main chambers have been left standing alone, and this has led to them being wrongly associated with the altars of the Druids.

Each tomb was walled and often roofed and constructed from massive unhewn stone blocks or slabs. These slabs of rock, set upright in the form of a chamber, were topped by a single huge capstone before being covered with stones and earth. Sometimes a ring of upright stones also surrounded these chambers. They must have looked awesome, set against a rugged background and the setting sun! In some of these tombs archaeologists have found a large number of human skeletons, plus flint arrowheads, stone axe-hammers and other weapons carefully chipped, shaped, and sometimes polished, together with coarsely made pottery. Sadly, over the years, many tombs have been robbed of their possessions and the stones used for other purposes.

The ancient monuments on Môn are varied in design, indicating that groups of peoples from different origins or with different ideas have settled on the fertile land. For example, the small passage graves are similar to those found in Brittany and Ireland, whilst the box shaped structures are similar to those found in the Clyde region. Others cannot be classified because of vandalism.

The abundance of megalithic tombs on Ynys Môn indicates that the population during this period was dense. These tombs or cromlechs were used from the earliest times through to about 1,000 BC, and probably form the largest collection of such monuments in the country.

Bodowyr Burial Chamber, near Brynsiencyn, in the southern part of the island, is situated about three kilometres west-north-west of the new parish church of Llanidan. It may well have belonged to one of the earliest groups of chambered passage graves in North Wales. Although it has never been excavated, it is thought to be the remains of a simple passage grave made some five thousand years ago, one of a group of four of this type on Môn, and part of a sprinkling reaching from Brittany to the Northern Isles. The large mushroom-shaped capstone is now supported on three upright stones with the fourth lying horizontal. Originally a small cairn or mound of stones would have covered the tomb. Access to the tomb would have been gained through a small passage, with a low sill-stone on the east side marking the position of the entrance.

In contrast, one of the most fully excavated chambered tombs on the island is situated two and a half kilometres south-east of Holyhead, between the A5 and B4545. Trefignath burial chamber is well sign-posted, and is laid out in such a way that the visitor can appreciate the main outlines of its long and complex history. Before excavation took place between 1977 and 1979, it was assumed that it had been constructed as a single 'gallery' grave, divided into segments. However, the most important discovery was that it comprised of three separate chambers, each built at a different phase of occupation. At the western end is the earliest chamber which dates from between 3,700 BC to 3,500 BC. The box like structure, once surrounded by a mound of stones, has been interpreted as a simple passage grave of a type found in several regions of Europe.

Later, at an unknown date, the tomb was enlarged by the construction of the central chamber, and then extended into a large wedge shape, with a deep recessed forecourt. The resulting design, similar to that found in megalithic tombs in the Severn Cotswold region, represents perhaps a new population or contacts with the south-west of Scotland.

Finally the grave was again extended by a third chamber to the east of the site. Its 'horn' shaped forecourt is clearly visible. Trefignath Burial Chamber probably served as a collective burial tomb and it appears that the final closure was made around 2,250 BC. However it continued to be used as a single monument, and may have been used, like so many others on Môn, for ritual and ceremonial purposes as well as a tomb for the dead. The chamber remained intact until the 19th century, but by the 1870's the former covering of stones and earth was all that remained. Today there is little to be seen of the mound.

Another tomb, similar to Bodowyr and Trefignath, is Tŷ Newydd Burial Chamber, which is in a dilapidated state. This site is situated near the village of Llanfaelog near Rhosneigr, and can be found by taking the A4080 for about seven hundred and fifty metres, turn left and continue for about six hundred and fifty metres past a right turn, where you will see the tomb sign-posted. You will need to climb a stile and walk along the edge of the field to arrive at the site. The narrow capstone is supported by two built-up pillars inserted in 1935 because a crack in the cover stone had widened. However, the stone may be only a fractured remnant of the original, as it is claimed that it split when a fire was lit on top of it to celebrate a birthday at the neighbouring farm. A second chamber is believed to have stood beside it, but no trace remains. Despite its poor condition this chamber is of interest, and may belong to the earliest megalithic period on Môn. The first excavations in 1936 revealed that the capstone had slipped to the north, and no longer covered the whole chamber. The chamber floor was covered in a layer of black earth and charcoal. This contained one hundred and ten pieces of broken quartz, a fine barbed and pointed flint arrow head, and some fragments of pottery. The entire tomb would have been covered with a circular cairn, and its hill top position suggests links with simple passage graves. From this information it can be dated to about 3,500 BC, placing it in the same period as Bodowyr and Trefignath.

Another intriguing monument is Din Dryfol, which can be reached by taking the A5 from the junction with the A5114, (Llangefni road) Head west for about four kilometers; turn left at a signpost for Tre-gof caravan site. Turn right at the next two T junctions, and then take the first left to get to Fferam Rhosydd. If you are driving, park carefully in a farm lane and follow the signpost across two fields, through a kissing gate on to a rocky hill. Din Dryfol Burial Chamber is situated on a narrow ledge at the foot of this hill. A huge cover stone survives at the eastern end, and marks the entrance to what would appear to have been a series of up to four rectangular chambers stretching twelve metres behind. The whole would have been covered by a long narrow cairn, probably as long as sixty-one metres, and would have taken many man-hours of effort to construct. Excavations have shown that, as with Trefignath, there were several periods of construction. During the earliest period the entrance posts to one of the chambers were built of wood. This is a very unusual combination for the period, although it has been suggested that this may have been more common in Stone Age times than first believed.

An interesting feature of the ruined chambered tomb at Plas Newydd, near the village of Llanedwen, is the presence of a vertical sill entrance with two semicircular holes on the upper edge, similar to those in stocks of the Middle Ages. It is possible that these cavities were partly natural in origin, and the stones chosen for their existence. However, it is impossible to know if a second stone, with corresponding holes, was used. Although the Plas Newydd chamber does resemble megalithic tombs in England, the purpose of these holes remains a mystery. These were superstitious times, and it has been suggested that they represent a false entrance to a closed chamber and were placed there to attract the attention of evil spirits who wished to harm the body of the deceased. Once inside, the spirit was trapped, thus keeping the tomb contents safe.

Lligwy Burial Chamber has the largest capstone on the island, and is worth a visit. It can be found on the A5025 just south-west of the village of Moelfre. The tomb is 1km along the road on the left. It can be seen from the road or visited by passing through a kissing gate into a field. The monument measures five and a half metres by four and a half metres and weighs twenty-eight tonnes, and looks like a giant flat mushroom. It is supported, half a metre above the ground, on eight low upright blocks which sit on a crude dry-stone walling. Beneath is an irregular pit, which appears to be a natural fissure in the rock as there is no formal layout to this chamber. The entrance was probably through the widest part to the east, and it is thought likely that, because of the position of the entrance, the Neolithic people who erected these tombs were sun worshippers. Excavations in 1909 revealed two burial sites separated by what appears to be rough paving. The bones of between fifteen and thirty men, women and children have been unearthed, together with mussel shells, pottery, flint tools and a bone pin.

The burial rites that took place at these different types of monuments were complicated. They would involve ceremonies in which bones would have been removed from partly decomposed bodies and moved around within the different sections of the monument as well as the entrance passage. As yet, the purpose of such practises is unknown to modern man.

Like many of the ancient sites in Wales there is a legend attached to Cromlech Lligwy. Tradition relates that one day a fisherman, whilst seeking shelter within the cromlech from a violent storm, fell asleep and dreamt that someone was struggling in the water of Lligwy Bay. The dream was so vivid that the man woke suddenly and rushed down to the sea. There, much to his amazement he saw a strange woman struggling to reach the land but unable to do so because of the high waves. The fisherman did not think of his own safety, but dived straight into the sea to rescue the lady. As he carried her to the shore he saw that she was a beautiful maiden dressed in a white robe and wearing jewelled bracelets. As he was about to set her down on the beach she asked him to carry her to 'the great stone.' When they reached the cromlech, she spoke again to the fisherman. 'If I had turned out to be an old hag, dressed in rags, you would have not saved me from the water.' Before the fisherman had time to reply she continued. 'I am a witch. I was in a ship passing the bay when the crew threw me overboard. I saw you resting in the great stone, and knew you were my only chance of survival. I disguised myself and, thanks to you, I am here to tell the tale. Now one good turn deserves another.' She stretched out her hand to the fisherman and he noticed that in the palm of her hand she held a small golden ball. 'I give you this golden ball which contains a snake-skin charm. As long as you keep it safe, well hidden from prying eyes, and allow no one to find it, good fortune will go with you always. Once a year you must take the golden ball, with the snake-skin inside it, and go down to the rocks and dip it into the sea. Then you must return it to its secret hiding place. If you lose it, or take the snake-skin out, your good luck will change.' And with these words the beautiful maiden disappeared. For a while the fisherman stood, hardly believing what he had just witnessed. Then he ran down to the shore and was in time to see the lady leap into a strange boat and sail away.

For a while the fisherman prospered. Then one day as he was dipping the golden ball into the sea as he had been told, it slipped from his hand and disappeared into the sea. From that moment on his luck changed. The fisherman spent days searching the shoreline looking for the golden ball, until one day he found it in a pool at low tide. He was delighted and carried it home and placed it in its secret hiding place. From that moment on his luck changed, and it is claimed that prosperity return to him, his children and his children's children.

There is also an amusing incident told of Lligwy chamber. It is said that, about a century ago, a farm servant was heard to say that he had heard that treasure was hidden near the cromlech, and that night he was going to dig for it. Another man overheard this conversation and decided to play a trick on the treasure seeker. As soon as it was dusk he went to the chamber, dug a hole in the ground, and pressed a pot into the earth leaving the impression that a pot had been removed. He then wrapped himself in a sheet and hid nearby. Presently the treasure seeker arrived at the site and shone his torch onto the ground to find a suitable spot to start digging. We can imagine his dismay when he discovered the hole, and realised that someone had been there before him. Slowly the prankster, wrapped in his white sheet, came towards him. The treasure seeker threw down his lamp and tools and fled as fast as his legs could take him. It is not recorded what he thought of his 'ghostly' encounter!

CHAPTER THREE

LATE NEOLITHIC FARMERS

For some reason, by 3,000 BC, many of the densely populated parts of southern Britain were in a period of decline. The causewayed settlements were abandoned and no new long barrows were being built. However, the scene was rather different in the west of Britain and in Scotland. Here the small settlements grew in size and the burial chambers built in earlier periods continued to be used and to be extended.

Archaeological evidence suggests that these tombs may have been used for social, symbolic and political functions, as well as a resting place for the dead. Although we still have much to learn about their lifestyle, we do know that these later Neolithic farmers were religious people who believed in an afterlife. These vaults are thought to have been used for many hundreds of years to symbolise the continuity and permanence of a particular clan, and were often enlarged or altered to suit the cultural needs of the community, as well as to accommodate other generations.

A new series of tombs were also being developed. These round barrows, as they are known, were highly regionalised and are a development of the earlier passage grave. The inspiration for these may have come from Ireland as many have designs typical to those found in the Boyne Valley. These circular monuments gradually began to replace the long structures, and also new ceremonial monuments, such as henges and stone circles, began to be erected.

Cremation burials replaced inhumations – the burial of the unburnt corpse – and also a new type of pottery, known as grooved ware, appeared. The pottery, distinctive because of its wicker basket decoration, evolved in Spain during the latter part of the Neolithic period, probably from small baskets or vessels made from esparto grass. The ornamental horizontal bands on the pottery are typical of the Spanish 'zone' pots and beakers, and are reminiscent of the hoops which formed the framework of the woven model.

One of the most important burial chambers in Môn from this period, and certainly the most impressive, is Barclodiad y Gawres, which is situated at Llanfaelog, on a headland overlooking Trecastell Bay. Cars must be left at Trecastell Bay car park, and visitors must take the path through the kissing gate to the end of the headland, which is approximately four hundred metres away. The tomb is locked. At the time of writing, the key can be obtained from the Wayside Cafe for a deposit of £5. Please do check details of the key-keeper as the holder may change.

You should take a torch with you to appreciate the spectacular designs on some of the stones.

During the 18th century the site was used as a 'stone' quarry and by the early 19th century many of the stones had been stolen or used to build walls in the area. A great deal of damage was done before excavation took place during 1952-1953. The late Professor T Powell and Glyn Daniel found that the central chamber is of a normal Neolithic type, and was probably the scene of many a funeral, or magical ritual connected with the religion of the day. The remains of two individuals were found during excavation. Scattered amongst the ashes of the hearth fire were the contents of either a 'witches' stew or a magic potion that had probably been thrown onto the central hearth. This foul brew contained whiting, eels, frogs, toads, snakes, snails, mice and shrew, and could not have been intended for human consumption. Instead it may provide us with the first evidence of truth, founded on ancient magic, in the folklore concerning the contents of a witches cauldron.

As we look at these remnants we can imagine the Neolithic clan, sweat pouring down their painted weather beaten bodies, as they danced around in a wild frenzy trying to communicate with the spirits and gods they worshipped.

Leading from the central chamber is a single chamber on one side and a double one on the other. Each would have been covered with a capstone, but only one, on the south side, now survives. In the undisturbed west side, cremated bones of a further two men were discovered, together with a long bone pin. What makes this chamber so remarkable is the discovery of a large amount of mural art. Five upright stones have chevrons, spirals and zigzags carved on their surfaces. It is thought that these designs were made by lightly pecking the surface with a hard stone chisel, no easy feat when you consider the primitive tools available. These markings were probably of special ritual and symbolic significance to the tomb builders but, as yet, unintelligible to modern man. One guess is that the decoration represents, in pattern form, an image of a Mother goddess, whose origins goes back via Ireland and Iberia to the Mediterranean. The designs have many similarities with those found in Spain and Portugal and give us some indication from which direction this particular group came. Thankfully, now that man has learned to respect his heritage, the chamber has been carefully restored, and a concrete dome built to protect its precious contents from the weather and vandals. This mirrors the original, which would have been constructed with a combination of rubble and turves spanning almost twenty-seven metres in diameter.

Pant-y-saer Neolithic chamber situated near the village of Benllech is also well known; yet today it is often used as a rubbish dump. This site can be found off the B5108 Benllech-Brynteg road by following the signposted raised footpath. The chamber was first excavated in 1875 and again in 1932. Sadly the limestone, of which it is built, is beginning to crumble, the capstone has tilted to the east, and the stone on the west side is missing. For unknown reasons the front had been previously closed by a large slab. The remains of a total of fifty-four men, women and children, including nine full term foetuses were discovered, along with a few scraps of broken pottery. The large number of burials suggests that the chamber was used over a long period of time. An offering of pottery, placed against the front of the chamber, suggests that ceremonies of remembrance, or funeral feasts, had taken place in the forecourt.

Môn lays claim to one of the best preserved, and most famous, chambered tombs in Britain; Bryn-celli-ddu. It is situated on the south of the island, and is probably one of the last megalithic tombs to be built on the island. It can be approached by turning off the A5 at Llanfair Pwllgwyngyll and travelling along the A4080 for about four kilometres. To the right is a minor road leading to Llanddaniel-fab. Just before reaching the village a signposted track, which is unsuitable for cars, leads to the chamber. At the end of the lane, the visitor will find a farm where a Department of Environment leaflet can be purchased and the key to the chamber obtained for a small fee. At first glance it looks like a miniature of the great burial mounds of the Boyne valley in Ireland, but on closer examination it can be seen to be nearer in style to those in Brittany. It was first excavated in 1928, when its long and complicated history began to unravel. It is likely that this tomb superseded a much earlier 'henge' monument, similar to the more spectacular Stonehenge in Wiltshire. The enclosure was marked by a wide ditch which probably had an outer bank. Inside the ditch there would have been a circular group of stone pillars, only two of which remain unbroken. At a later date the henge was deliberately wrecked and concealed by the builders of the impressive passage grave. Perhaps there was a clash of cultures.

Once inside the fenced enclosure, a partly restored circular mound is visible which enables the visitor to gain a view of what the original, some twenty-four metres across, must have looked like. The locked iron door leads to the passage grave, in which the central chamber contains a free-standing smooth faced stone pillar. On the south wall, one of the stones has a carved spiral design which is generally accepted to be of symbolic relevance. Some historians believe that these marking represent the endless wanderings of water, or some mythical river. Others believe that it could symbolise the snake; a symbol of vitality to these Neolithic farmers. Or perhaps it represents a map for a spiritual journey?

Bones, both burnt and unburnt, were found in the central chamber as well as in the passage chamber. At the feet of the dead were placed quartz pebbles. In the centre was the remains of a fire pit, which contained a human ear bone. When the tomb was finally sealed, the outer passage was systematically blocked with earth and stones.

We can only guess that the forecourt may have been used for elaborate ceremonial rites during a major festival, because a small ox was found buried in an enclosed stone and timber frame. Also, on the outside of the mound at the back of the chamber, is a cast of a stone which would have originally marked the centre of a pre-existing circle. The original, which can be seen in the National Museum of Wales at Cardiff, has fascinating spirals and decorative patterns carved on it, and is likely to have witnessed some important pagan rituals. Who knows? The builders of the passage grave may have replaced some central feature of the henge with their own rituals, which in turn may have been covered by the large mound over the tomb to keep out prying eyes. Although Bryn-celli-ddu is only sixteen kilometres from Barclodiad y Gawres, it is thought to have been built by people following a different culture.

When one considers that the original mound would have covered the whole of the area now fenced in, it is easy to realise that, besides being used for burials, this must have been a very important meeting place, in much the same way as Stonehenge. Although this is a New Stone Age or Neolithic site dating from 3,000 BC, it continued to be used throughout the Bronze Age, and is regarded today as much a Bronze Age as a Neolithic site.

To understand the significance of these burial chambers, perhaps we need to look upon them not merely as burial chambers but as churches for the gods of the living and the dead. These people were governed by the agricultural year, and the changing seasons would have assumed a special significance to them. Like the people of today, they would have celebrated midwinter (Christmas), the sowing season (Easter), midsummer (Ascension) and harvest (Michaelmas).

Probably, for the first time, man saw the production of food as a symbol of man and nature. Man had to plough, sow and reap in the right order so that the earth could shape itself into new life. They believed that when man died he too turned into earth, and so the cycle of fertility repeated endlessly. Perhaps one day we will learn the true secrets of these people, as well as the significance of magnificent sites such as these.

CHAPTER FOUR

BRONZE AGE

Around 2,500 BC Môn was slowly being encroached by yet another band of people, this time from northern and eastern Europe, most particularly from Holland and around the Rhine. They probably crossed over the shallow channel from France to land along the southern coasts of Britain. Gradually they travelled inland and some made their way, over a period of time, to Môn. Others would have travelled around the Welsh coast to West and South Wales. They were taller than the Iberians, with fairer hair, grey eyes, and a rounded head. They were also more powerful and spoke a sort of Indo-European language. They became known as the Beaker Folk, a name derived from the bell-shaped pottery beakers that were found amongst their valued grave goods. Fragments of their pottery show that they were of a high quality, and elaborately decorated with incised patterns made by using a bird's wing bone as a chisel. Others that were decorated with multiple chevrons are more rare. These beakers may also have been used, as the name implies, as a personal drinking vessel to hold barley wine or mead. On the death of the owner, the beaker would be buried with him and filled with a herb flavoured alcoholic drink, which they believed would help to sustain the deceased on the journey to the next world. It was a hard existence, and life expectancy was short. The average male lived for twenty-five years, and many children died in infancy. However, as remains of both long and rounded headed people have been found in chambered and barrow tombs, it is agreed that the two races must have lived a peaceful co-existence. They may even have inter-married and combined cultural traditions, in much the same way as ethnic groups mingle with in the British culture of today.

By now the discovery of the wheel and the development of the plough had transformed the landscape. Early ploughs would have comprised of little more than a forked stick, but as more knowledge and better skills were acquired, more advanced implements were made. These would have been pulled by oxen, the yoke being lashed to the animals' horns rather than placed over its shoulders. Also, studies of the soil indicate that these people had learnt to use manure to improve their crop production.

Whereas Neolithic settlements were centred on the lowlands, the early Bronze Age peoples moved into the uplands where circular huts, much smaller than the Neolithic long houses, have been found amongst low-walled enclosed fields. This shift to higher ground may have been due to three factors: An increase in population; exhausted lowland farming; and an improvement in the climate at higher levels.

These new settlers would have lived in crude huts, taking over and adapting many of the established Neolithic settlements for their own needs. They grouped together in small villages, and protected themselves against raiding parties from adjacent villages or from across the Irish sea by building a single ditch around the settlement.

One of these adapted sites is Castell Bryn-gwyn, which is located near the village of Brynsiencyn off the A4080. The site is well signposted, and it is possible to drive to the site, although the lanes are narrow. Today, little more than a single bank remains which stands some four metres high enclosing a circular area of about fifty-five metres in diameter. This area was excavated in 1959-60 and revealed a long and complicated history, which is still open to much discussion. It appears that the earliest monument was raised in the late Neolithic or early Bronze Age period, and comprised of a bank with an external ditch. Some historians consider it to be a henge monument as the remains of a stone circle stands within a ditch and outer bank, some two hundred metres away. Later the site was reused and a timber-riveted rampart, with a deep V-shaped ditch on the outside, was erected. There is also some documented reference to a castle built in the 11th century by King Olaf, grandfather of Gruffudd ap Cynan, somewhere near the Menai Straits. Historians have attempted to link this with Castell Bryn-gwyn, but again no evidence exists to confirm this.

The Bronze Age is traditionally marked as the introduction of metal-making and, although it played a vital role in man's development, little is known of its beginnings. We know that the Age of Copper started in south east Europe, and did not catch on in Britain until nearly 2,000 years later. Here the natives were content to copy, in flint, those copper items that they had seen. Objects made of copper first appeared in graves in the south of England from 3,000 BC, but it is evident that these people were users rather than manufacturers. The earliest items found were axes, daggers and awls which could have been imported from other parts of Europe, and were only marginally better than the stone tools used previously.

However, across the sea in Ireland copper working had commenced as distinctive axes from this period have been found. Also a wooden trackway was discovered recently in Corlea, and has marks which could only have been made with a metal tool, thus proving that the timbers were felled around 2,260-2,250 BC.

However, when it was discovered that a much stronger metal could be made by mixing copper and tin the Bronze Age rapidly caught on in Britain. It is believed that the late Neolithic people, who evolved into the

Bronze Age races, were aggressive by nature. It has often been stated that they were interested in making wars, and that the lure of dazzling metal war weapons attracted them, but we have no evidence to support this.

However, we do know that around this time Wales, and particularly Môn, found itself at the centre of an expanding export market for Irish metal goods and it is possible that Caergybi (Holyhead) became the centre of this trade. On the lower south-western slopes of Mynydd Caergybi stand Cytiau'r Gwyddelod (the huts of the Irish), but despite its name there is no known connection with Ireland. The settlement was inhabited from the Late Neolithic period through to the Roman period. It was probably first built at the time that trade with Ireland began, hence the name. Who knows? Perhaps this was one of the main trading centres for Irish goods?

It appears that the rich copper deposits in Kerry were used to their full potential, and we can only assume that during this time there was much trading between Ireland and the Cornish tin mines. The Irish produced high quality goods which must have caused as much excitement then as those produced by Faberge at the end of the 19th century.

As yet, the British people had not mastered the art of metal making and we can imagine the interest generated as news of these fine products travelled along the trading routes. We can also assume that anyone who wanted to impress would buy an ornament or weapon made of Irish bronze – similar to a modern day status symbol. It is also possible that the myth about the Neolithic people's love of war developed from this desire to own a fine crafted exquisite weapon.

Eventually ore, which came mainly from the Wicklow Hills in Ireland, was worked into sheets which were exported to Britain and the continent. Under the influence of the Irish traders, the native settlers were eager to learn to make metal artefacts for themselves. Soon it became the fashionable trade of the day, and we can imagine that every settlement had its own 'expert' craftsman who would make items to order. No doubt there was much competition as each clan vied with the next, and displayed their 'best' pieces. Although goods would have been costly to produce, we can surmise that every young man would dream of owning an ornate dagger or impressing his loved one with the gift of a bronze pin, brooch or trinket.

Although there is little evidence in support of this, it is also highly likely that at this time local people became aware of the copper deposits on Parys mountains, and used it to their advantage. The only known Bronze Age copper mines in Europe which can be visited, are not far away. At the Great Orme Mines in Llandudno the visitor can see extensive workings and gain an unique picture of the working life of a Bronze Age labourer. Visitors are encouraged to first see an introductory video and talk to excavators, before seeing the limestone cliffs in which the veins of green malachite and blue azurite are clearly visible.

As more knowledge was gained and skills were passed on, the Bronze Age slowly established itself and archaeologists have discovered that, like previous Ages, different societies with their own unique cultures and rituals lived during the period. Amongst the innovations from the Late Bronze Age was the introduction from the continent of various types of razor and tweezer. However, only three specimens have been recorded in Wales, one of which was a double-leaf type Bronze tweezer, that is thought to have been used for plucking hair. From this find we can assume that our ancestors were beginning to take more of an interest in their appearance. Gold torcs from the late Bronze Age, in the form of necklets, armlets or waist-belts of twisted metal, have also been found. Some were wound spirally, obviously for use as armlets, whilst others were too awkward for personal ornaments. Their purpose is not clear, but it has been suggested that they may have been used as girdles for large wooden idols, or to protect the wearer from evil spirits in times of need. It has also been suggested that they were a symbol of infinity, or of the never-ending cycle of death and rebirth. Only time will reveal more.

In 1856 eleven armlets were found at Gaerwen, together with two small bands consisting of two thin hollow plates of gold joined by a central band which were possibly used as earrings or, as suggested more recently, hair ornaments. Two bracelets with slightly cupped terminals were found near Beaumaris, and can now be seen in the British Museum in London.

CHAPTER FIVE

STANDING STONES AND THE STORY OF BEDD BRANWEN

During the Bronze Age, burial methods changed. Instead of placing their dead in large stone tombs like earlier settlers, the Bronze Age people became involved in using a much wider range of monuments. These were linked by a circular plan, and are similar to the Bryn-celli-ddu site mentioned in chapter two. The dead were buried singly in stone cists or coffins, often covered with a barrow or mound of earth. The barrows varied in design, with or without kerbstones, and sometimes surrounded by a ditch or circular arrangement of stones. The body was placed on its side and in a crouched position. Alongside was placed the distinctive beaker, a few weapons, and some tools to represent personal wealth.

Whichever method was used it was clear that Bronze Age man had a well-developed system of burial, although the rituals of death would appear to have been less important than in the Neolithic period. The majority of the cairns are to be found in the central forested region and not in the limestone areas previously occupied by the Neolithic people. This was possibly because the climate had changed from being dry with warm summers to being cold and damp.

We are not sure of the religious beliefs of the Bronze Age people, but it is thought that, unlike the Neolithic people who worshipped the earth, they believed in a sky god, possibly the sun. It is likely that they would have held their religious meetings in or around the ceremonial stone circles. Sadly none of these have survived on Môn although a few may be seen in the uplands of Meirionnydd.

Another interesting feature of the Bronze Age are the maen hir, or standing stones. These are generally accepted by archaeologists as ritual, perhaps linked to the more elaborate stone circles. As such, they may provide us with some insight into a civilization that was concerned with the forces of life and nature. We can assume that, in part at least, both the stone circles and individual stones were probably related to major events, such as the changing of the seasons or the movement of heavenly bodies. It appears that the rising and setting of the sun and moon interested many communities. Perhaps these circles were an astronomical clock, laid out with such exactness that skilled practitioners could, by noting the position of the sun, moon and stars, acquire knowledge of seasons or directions when travelling.

In southern Britain, the Beaker people were responsible for building the great 'henge' monuments of Avebury and Stonehenge. Until the 1960's, Castell Bryn-gwyn was thought to have been such a site, but excavations revealed that its ditch was more defensive than ritual.

Most impressive are the two standing stones at Penrhos Feilw, which are situated about two kilometres from Holyhead. Oddly, a pair of standing stones is rare in North Wales, but common in South Wales. The Penrhos Feilw stones are almost identical in size and shape, and stand about three metres tall and over three metres apart. Although never properly excavated, tradition relates that a large stone coffin containing human bones, arrowheads and spearheads was found in the centre of the circle between the two stones. This might suggest that they were erected in honour of an important person within the tribe or clan, although there is no evidence of this is.

Carreg y Lleidr, (the robber stone), is situated on private property at Llanerchymedd, and resembles a man with a pack on his back. According to legend the man stole some books, including a bible, from the parish church. As he sneaked across the field with his sack of books slung over his shoulder he was turned into stone.

Tregwehelydd standing stone, which stands isolated in a field north east of Bodedern, near Llanddeusant, is prominently positioned on the crest of a ridge. Standing at almost three metres high it is impressive but, although under the care of CADW, it is in poor condition with the three pieces held together by bolts and bands.

Another group of standing stones that are of interest to the visitor is the Llanfechell 'triangle', situated on a hilltop just north of Llanfechell village. It can be reached from four directions, but the easiest is from the Cemaes-Llanfechell Road. Once the visitor reaches the Caemaes roundabout, leave the car and take the unmarked footpath, which includes steps over a wall besides Tyddyn Paul Cottage. Keep to the right of the wall until the standing stones come into sight – a five to ten minute walk. Although the site is difficult to access, the view from the stones is well worth the effort. The three stones, each over two metres in height, stand in an unique triangular arrangement, three metres apart. Surprisingly, despite their unusual order, no legend has been woven around them.

On Môn alone there are the remains of, or records of, thirty-nine standing stones. Some historians believe them to be markers for cemeteries and, although their existence remains a mystery their abundance and prominent positions indicate that they were of vital significance to our ancestors.

Around 1,500 BC, during what we now call the mid-Bronze Age, cremation came into practice. The ashes of the dead were emptied into a leather bag or an ornamental earthenware urn or vase, and buried. These urns were sometimes placed in an inverted position, and usually protected by a stone coffin covered with a mound of earth. Some burial goods have been found including bronze axes, other highly polished weapons and tools, bronze and gold ornaments, and more advanced pottery.

Several single graves under one round barrow were by this time common throughout Britain. Those of important people again contained fine objects, including metal work, beautifully made flint-work, and decorated pottery.

The Bronze Age Llanddyfnan cemetery, at Pentraeth, is interesting because of the combination of a standing stone and round barrows. All the monuments are on private land, but are easily seen on the right-hand side of the B5109 Pentraeth-Llangefni Road. To the left, as you look, is the largest barrow which is best seen from the west against the sky. This barrow was excavated at the beginning of the century and seven Bronze Age cremation burials were found. There appears to be no central burial, but one individual obviously was wealthier than the others. Pottery, a razor, and a decorated bracelet suggest contacts with Scotland and Ireland, whereas the axe and knife came from southern Britain. All these objects are now on display in the National Museum of Wales in Cardiff.

A second barrow in this group was excavated in 1908, and interestingly contained the bones of one person who had been buried in a boat-shaped pit grave. This individual burial, and the shape of the grave, may well pre-date the main barrow, and suggests that the deceased may have belonged to the founding family of this community.

Another notable round barrow burial chamber is Bedd Branwen, at Llanddeusant, which is famous for its associations with the fabled Branwen. She was the daughter of Llyr and is featured in those delightful tales, Y Mabinogi, a collection of stories that portray a mythical and colourful world. They were first written down in 1300 in Llyfr Gwyn Rhydderch (The White Book of Rhydderch), and again in Llyfr Coch Hergest (The Red Book of Hergest) between 1382 and 1410. Today, Llyfr Gwyn Rhydderch is preserved in The National Museum of Wales, and Llyfr Coch Hergest at Jesus College in Oxford.

The site of Bedd Branwen can be found by travelling north-east from Llanddeusant Church to the cross-roads with a chapel; turn right and take the second farm road on the left, opposite the water installation. Proceed down the lane, which is a public footpath, for seven hundred and fifty metres to a field gate on the right hand side, just short of a wood. The edge of the barrow is situated where the power line of an electricity pole changes direction. Again it is situated on a private field, but the owner allows access when the field is not in use for growing hay or other crops.

According to the Mabinogion story, Branwen died of a broken heart as she wept beside Afon Alaw over the trouble she had inadvertently caused between the warriors of Wales and Ireland. The story goes that one day Brân (or Bendigeidfran fab Llyr), the giant king of Britain, was sitting with one of his brothers on a rock at Harlech when he noticed a fleet of thirteen ships approaching from Ireland. The fleet belonged to Matholwch, the Irish king, who had come to ask the permission of the brothers to marry their sister Branwen. There was much rivalry between Britain and Ireland at the time so Brân readily agreed to the marriage, hoping it would unite the two countries. The kings, with their courtiers, set sail for the royal palace at Aberffraw in Môn. Here they celebrated the wedding with a grand feast. Tents were set up and people came from miles around. No expense was spared and all day they wined and dined. Brân had a younger, quarrelsome, half-brother called Efnysien, who knowing nothing of the marriage, was surprised when by chance he came across the encampment. In a temper he drew his dagger and maimed the Irish horses one by one. Matholwch was furious and ordered his soldiers to strike camp immediately. On hearing about the incident Brân tried to make amends for Efnysien's deeds and offered the Irish king gifts of silver, gold and horses. Finally he offered his most treasured possession, Y Pair Dadeni, a magic cauldron that restored dead troops to life but left them speechless. The king accepted the gifts and, after much hand shaking, sailed back to Ireland with his bride.

For a year Branwen was held in high esteem in the Irish court. The couple were happy and a son was born. However the king could not forget his brother-in-law's actions and placed an embargo on trade with Britain, and imprisoned any 'foreigner' who ventured into Ireland. Finally he divorced Branwen and put her to work in the palace kitchens where she slaved for three years. Whilst working there, she trained a starling to carry a message across the sea to her brother, Brân. Eventually he received a message and set out to invade Ireland and rescue his sister. Legend has it that Irish coastguards reported seeing a mountain and a forest coming across the sea towards the river Shannon. In fact, what they saw was Brân, who was too big to board a ship, walking beside his fleet across the sea. On his arrival peace talks began and, after much discussion, Matholwych reluctantly agreed to abdicate in favour of his young son. With this Efnysien again displayed his true character and picked up the child and threw him into the fire. A cruel war followed, in which the Irish put the cauldron to good use by throwing in the corpses and restoring them to life. Efnysien, seeking to end the trouble he had started, successfully ended the battle by jumping into the cauldron and willing his heart to explode thus breaking the cauldron.

At the end of the battle, only seven Welsh warriors remained. Brân himself was wounded in the foot by a poisoned spear and ordered his men that, on his death, they were to cut off his head, take it back to Britain and bury it in Llundain (London), facing towards France because no invader would land on British soil as long as his head was buried there. It is claimed that his head was buried where the Tower of London stands today.

After the small band of followers had arrived back in Môn, Branwen sat down by the Afon Alaw and died of a broken heart. It is claimed that she was buried at Bedd Branwen. However, Bedd Branwen monument is much older than any known version of this story but who knows how many generations had related the legends of y Mabinogi before they were ever written. The centre stone was erected at the end of 3,000 BC, and the burial mound was built around 2,000 BC to form a cemetery for up to twelve people. These were evidently wealthy people as they were buried with fascinating imported objects, which are worth seeing at Bangor Museum. Excavation in 1966 revealed that the mound was of a complex construction. The centre stone had stood as an independent memorial for some centuries before the site was used as a burial ground. Three urns containing cremated remains were found at Bedd Branwen, together with accompanying pots and other goods, and a ring of stones built over them. The whole area between the ring and the central stone was filled with overlapping slabs pitched towards the centre, and then covered in turves and soil extending to a kerb of boulders, some of which are visible today. Later, a further four cremated burials were added to the mounds.

There are some unusual features concerning the burial arrangements in this barrow. For example, unlike similar memorials, no one person was given a prime position and bodies were placed equally around the stone ring, irrespective of wealth or importance in the community. One man had a fine necklace of amber and carved imported jet beads, another just one jet bead. Interestingly, in contrast to other burial sites in Britain, no body was buried with a dagger. Another curiosity is the separate burial of the petrous temporal (ear) bones of infants, as yet an unexplained ritual found at several sites in North Wales. Three examples have been uncovered where pairs of ear-bones from a new-born child have been placed in small pots, and buried alongside an urn containing adult bones.

By 1,000 BC many of the uphill areas were in decline, with fields and settlements being abandoned in favour of the lower grounds. The reason for these changes is not known, but it may have been triggered by the onset of a colder and wetter climate which led to a shortening of the growing season. There were social changes too as large communities were forced to live in smaller areas. There was competition for the fertile lands, and we can safely assume that considerable tension and unrest developed. Overcrowded conditions would have led to disease and a shortage of food. New weapons were introduced which included swords and shields. Horse riding and wheeled chariots first appeared on the scene, and it is possible that survival was reserved for the strongest and fittest of the tribes.

Eventually society became more settled and rituals and customs crystallised into a more unified culture. It was into this more contented background that the Iron Age Celtic invaders arrived.

CHAPTER SIX

THE IRON AGE CELTS (the wider picture)

The oldest archaeological traces of the Celtic races can be found in the Austrian Alps at Halsatt near Salzburg. Here we can see the first evidence of iron-workings, the word 'iron' derives from the Celtic word 'isarnos.' It is these people who are credited with having introduced the Iron Age to Britain.

It has been traditionally accepted that the Iron Age spanned from about 600BC to the first century of the Christian Era, around 400 AD. It began when groups of Celtic immigrants invaded Britain and intermingled with, or subdued the Bronze Age people. The Celts were the first established large race in Europe but were increasingly under pressure, on the continent, from the expanding Germanic people and the Romans. The first Celtic settlers probably came to Britain of their own will at a very early date. Others came later along the established trading routes: some came from south-western Germany and Switzerland, and were descended from the people who created trade links with the Eastern Mediterranean and probably further afield; others came from central and southern Spain and settled in south Wales; yet more came from southern Germany and eastern France. There were two distinct groups of Celts, displaying basic differences in colouring, height and stature; but all were accepted as fearless warriors who liked bright colours and glittering ornamentation. They were also skilled craftsmen. The other basic difference between the two groups of Insular Celts (the Celts who lived on the islands of Britain) was purely linguistic. The Insular Celts had two dialects, or even languages, these being: Goidelic, which was the forerunner of Irish (Gaelic), Manx and Gaelic (of Scotland); the other was the Brythonic language, which was the direct ancestor of Welsh, Llydaweg (Breton) and Cerniweg (Cornish).

It has been widely thought that the Celts pushed most of the native people from Wales into Ireland, the Isle of Man and possibly into Scotland, and that the families that remained settled peacefully to live alongside the new lords of the manor. This view, like so many others to do with the Celts, must now be questioned. Radiocarbon dating and re-assessment of some archeological finds, show that many of the so called Iron Age hill-forts were actually built in the late Bronze Age, which means that the Celts and the Bronze Age age native inhabitants probably coexisted for longer than previously thought. Although we know that this was a period of unrest in northern and central Europe there is little to suggest a mass influx of people. The most likely explanation is that there was a gradual over-spill of people into Britain over a long period of time.

Between 400 BC and 250 BC a second influx of people, or their ideas, established the more characteristic Celtic culture that is renowned for its magnificent artwork. They came from La Tène, a Swiss settlement on Lake Lleuchâtel, where a large deposit of metal ware has been discovered. Artifacts such as bronze mirrors, horse brasses and chariot decorations from this period can be seen in many British and European museums today.

The early Celts were a volatile, militaristic race, who were constantly being pressed from the north and east by the Germanic tribes and the ever expanding Roman Empire. It was during the 4th century BC that they settled in northern Italy after invading Rome in 390BC. Their nomadic and warfaring nature took them on as far as Greece, where is was recorded that they invaded Delphi in 297 BC.

During the 2nd century the Roman military forces increased and conquered southern and central France before moving northwards and finally conquering Gallia Belgica in the middle of the first century BC. The Celts were forced further north, and it was during this time that most of them arrived in Britain, and established the thirty-three recorded communities.

However it is also possible that as early as 2,000 BC, tribes with Celtic origins already lived in Britain and Ireland to be joined gradually by traders and nomadic warriors from Europe. We know that the main tin trading route from Asia Minor to Cornwall, called the Phoenician Trading Route, had been in existence since pre-Roman times and we are almost certain that Celtic migrants came to Britain by this way. Incidentally, Cornwall during this period was the largest tin-producing area in the western World.

We are therefore not certain when, or indeed why, the Celts arrived in Britain, but we do know that they were experts at protecting themselves. What remains is an abundance of splendid hill-forts – almost six hundred in Wales alone, and approximately one fifth of the British total. It appears that, whereas the Neolithic and Bronze Age people spent a great deal of time building tombs for the dead, the Iron Age people preferred to concentrate their building efforts on communities for the living. Armed with basic equipment such as antler picks, oxen shoulder blades and wicker baskets, they set about changing the landscape by constructing massive walled settlements, some of which have lasted for two thousand five hundred years.

These hill-forts varied considerably in design and size, and represented the homes of a powerful thriving community. Some consisted of a series of round huts grouped together within an enclosure, which protected the occupants against unwanted intruders. Other sites have revealed the remains of foundations that contained streets of houses, laid out almost on present day town planning ideas The most remarkable of these is not far from Anglesey, at Tre'r Ceiri near the summit of Yr Eifl, about twenty kilometres south-west of Caernarfon. Today the surrounding wall, which is four metres high, stands as an impressive monument to the fort building skills of the Celts. Within this enclosure are the ruins of one hundred and fifty huts! At the other end of the scale, but equally as impressive are the smaller hill-forts that are balanced dangerously above vertical cliffs. In the next chapter we will visit some of the more interesting Iron Age sites on Anglesey.

At many of the hill-forts archaeological excavations have revealed evidence that iron smelting took place. The earliest iron object found in Wales is a sword dating from about 600 BC, which was discovered in Llyn Fawr above the Rhondda Valley in South Wales. It has been suggested that, thanks to the production of iron axes, the great oaks that once lined the valleys throughout Wales were felled to enable the land to be used for farming and the community. The abundance of fine Iron Age artistic and military artefacts that have been discovered could have been the equipment of an invading race, or ornate gifts exchanged between tribal chieftains, or perhaps they were part of the wide range of goods traded between continents since the early Bronze Age. Again only further studies and the continual re-assessment of the period will tell us more.

The Celts were a capable and clever race who brought a precise social order to Wales, which gradually evolved into a tribal system. They did what the 'men of Stone' and 'the men of Bronze' could not do. They became masters of the heavy clay soil, and battled with the wild and rugged land. Agriculture was the way of life for the common people of the Iron Age. They ploughed the fields and hewed down the trees. Within their hill-forts they established a ruling class with the main focus on loyalty to the clan rather than the tribe.

The noble clansmen believed they shared a common ancestor, even though that ancestor may have been mythical rather than human. Below them were the farmers who tilled the land and raised the livestock. Then came the craftsmen who made everyday life easier, and fashioned the goods prized by their superiors. The third group were the serfs or servants who worked as slaves for the clan. They were dependent on the clan for their survival and may have been captives or people who had arrived from outside the clan system for some other reason.

The success of each hill-fort was largely governed by the land that supplied their needs. Their wealth was measured by the droves of cattle, horses, swine and sheep they owned. Life centred around the seasonal calendar. At harvest-time the ears of corn were cut with iron sickles and brought to the village for cleaning and threshing, The husks were used for animal fodder, and the grain placed in stores with raised floors to allow the air to circulate. Later the animals were brought down from the upland pastures to forage the stubble in the field. This helped to break up the earth, and the animal's manure helped to replenish the fertile soil in time for the sowing season.

The Celts were expert in horsemanship and the chariot, which provided them with so much success on the battlefields. They decorated their horses and chariots with ornaments, and decked themselves in fine gold chased buckles, torcs and bracelets, which must have made an impressive sight as they glistened in the sunlight. It has been reported that these fearless warriors, woad smeared and often naked, sped into battle in their war chariots, hurling javelins at their enemy before dismounting and attacking them with swords. Some historians have compared Celts in battle with the Ancient Greek heroes of the Trojan Wars.

In Celtic mythology the horse was worshipped by Epona, the horse goddess. The Celts believed that the gods were able to appear in any animal form they chose, and several animals were considered sacred and regarded as 'totems.' For example the wild boar was a symbol of ferocity, and its spirit would make their warriors fierce in battle. However, overall 'Lord' of the animals was Cernunnos, the horned god, who was seen by the Celts as the ruler of the natural Kingdom.

Unlike the Bronze Age peoples, the Celts did not worship at Sun temples, but rather in the oak groves which they honoured as holy places. Here the Druids, or priests, built their altars. These forests, besides being of sacred significance, were also a rich source of wood for domestic and iron smelting fires; for timber to build huts, grain and cattle shelters; and for fences. The Celts were also known to have gathered twigs and small branches from other trees, such as elm and ash, which were then laid on drying racks. In winter the sun dried leaves were used to feed the animals.

The Celts were also extremely interested in natural wells, springs, pools and sources of rivers, and most probably believed these to be entrances to the underworld which is so prevalent in their mythology. With no great burial monuments to the Iron Age dead it has been suggested that, as water was so important to the Celtic culture, the rivers, lakes and wet areas became the final resting places for the dead. As we shall see later, Llyn Cerrig Bach was a sacred lake which possibly could have been a burial place for the dead. The graves of a few warriors and wealthy females have been found in central and southern England, but these are exceptional. None have been found in Môn or the remainder of north Wales.

Celtic mythology is also dominated by the cult of head hunting, which they considered to be the centre of strength and wisdom. The Iron Age Celts, unlike their Celtic Christian descendants, gloried in battle. When another tribe was defeated, the heads of some of the captives were severed from their bodies and taken back to the settlement where they would be embalmed in cedar oil and displayed on posts. They believed that the strength contained in these heads would assist them in future battles, and many such skulls have been discovered 'guarding' sacred wells, temples and shrines.

On the other hand, the Celts also had a close relationship with nature, and prayed to their gods in the oak groves where the Druids or priests built their altars. The warlords were advised by the Druids, and the young were taught to respect the rights of the individual, and to value family and tribal laws, customs and traditions. Music played an important role in their ceremonies, and attached to each order or tribe was a guild of bards, who knew the teachings of the Druids by heart.

CHAPTER SEVEN

IRON AGE SITES TO VISIT

One of the best known Iron Age settlements in Môn is the Tŷ Mawr group of huts at South Stack, Caergybi (Holyhead) which was first excavated in 1862-1868 by the Hon W O Stanley, a local landowner and MP, who did much to preserve the prehistory of Anglesey. On reaching Caergybi the visitor should follow signs for the ferry terminal and then for South Stack. At the cafe, park the car and walk along the signposted path. The site contains the remains of ten large, round stone huts and smaller rectangular buildings, which are scattered along the hillside, partly underground and entered by one or two steps.

Stanley's early excavations of the rectangular buildings uncovered hearths, slag, crushed quartz and evidence of metal workings indicating that they were used as workshops. However further excavations carried out in 1978-1982 found little evidence of industry, but provided more information about farming activities. With the aid of radiocarbon dating it has been established that the settlement was not, as Stanley suggested, a single village set up and abandoned during the Roman period, but rather a series of farmsteads of varying dates. There is evidence of occupation during the Middle Stone Age, Neolithic and Bronze Ages, but the buildings visible today definitely belong to the Iron Age and were probably used up to the 6th century AD. Nearby, at Ellen's Tower, you can visit an exhibition and learn more about the settlement.

The large defensive hill-fort of Caer-y-tŵr can be visited by taking a lengthy walk to the top of the rocky summit of Mynydd Caergybi, on which it sits. The visitor will be rewarded with superb views. But beware! Don't leave the pathways as the ample vegetation hides very rough surfaces. Although not accurately dated, there is little doubt that this is the remains of an Iron Age hill-fort, and very similar to others in North Wales. On the northern and eastern sides, the stone wall stands to a height of three metres in places and is about three metres thick, and wide enough to have included a rampart walk. It is constructed of dry-stone masonry with a rubble core, and the seventeen acre site has only one entrance, at the north-eastern corner. The south-western side overlooks a sheer precipice with no need for further protection. There are no visible signs of huts, which may indicate that it was used as a temporary refuge in times of trouble. Recent excavations at the highest point have revealed the base of a late Roman watchtower. As excellent views over Caergybi harbour are offered from the site, it could possibly have been used as a lookout station by the Iron Age Celts as well as the Romans.

Another coastal hill-fort that juts out into the sea is Dinas Gynfor at Cemaes. The promontory fort can be seen by taking the A5025 road from Amlwch in a westerly direction towards Llanbadrig Church. Ignore the sign for the church and continue for one kilometre until you reach the footpath sign. Park close to the verge and walk down towards the hill-fort which is linked to the mainland by a broad marshy causeway. Dinas Gynfor, especially the defence ramparts, are best seen from the path. Limited excavations have shown that the wall face at the south eastern side was built of stone dug from the quarry ditch, which is a rare feature in Welsh hill-forts. It is best to visit this site in winter as, in summer, the bracken can be high. The hill-fort is surrounded on all sides by steep cliffs, and during the 19th century the harbour was used to export china stone which had been quarried within the fort. The ruins on the shore belong to this industry and not to the hill-fort.

Two later sites that are worth a visit are Din Lligwy and Caer Leb. Both these are believed to be from the Romano-Brythonic period, but may well have been founded earlier and re-occupied later. Din Lligwy enclosed hut group is at Moelfre, and is the largest hill-fort site in Môn. Cars must be left at Llanallgo, north of Benllech, and from there a mile walk in a northerly direction through a wood will take the visitor to the site. A burial chamber that dates back to the Neolithic period, and mentioned earlier, is reached first. A little further along is the well hidden Celtic village, where the most infertile of minds will be fired with vivid scenes of village activity. Din Lligwy is not the usual type of Iron Age fort, but rather a native village which seems to have been fortified at a later stage, possibly when the Romans invaded the island. The site could well have been one of the chief Celtic settlements on the island, and is enclosed by walls which are approximately one and a half metres thick and shaped like a pentagon. Neat white buildings would appear to have belonged to a small estate, with workshop buildings and houses. Although described as a hut group, some historians have compared this site to the Romanised villas found in the south of England. Excavations have revealed evidence of earlier occupation, but the date of the changes that resulted in the present grouping of buildings is uncertain. Once inside the enclosure the visitor will notice a large house in the right-hand corner. This was clearly the main domestic building and reveals some repair by the owner. A silver ingot, imported pottery, and even glassware, have been found on the site. Another round building to the south of the enclosure was also a domestic quarter, but it appears that the two large rectangle buildings were used as workshops. Rows of iron working hearths and deposits of slag, indicate that this was once a well established iron smelting workshop. It has been suggested that Din Lligwy was a local centre for smithing and the inhabitants took advantage of the Roman invasion to derive much of their wealth from bartering their products with the Roman military centres.

The settlement and defended enclosure of Caer Lêb, is surrounded by imposing banks and deep water-filled ditches. It can be found near the village of Brynsiencyn, and is well signposted. Park on the verge, but be careful as the ground in autumn and winter is boggy. The site was partially excavated in 1866, when the footings of a rectangular building were found against the inner rampart, and a round hut was discovered in the southern part of the enclosure. Finds included pottery from the 2nd, 3rd and 4th centuries but, as with many of the other sites, this could have been occupied during an earlier phase. Along the road, beside Pont Sarn Las (bridge), approximately five hundred metres north-east, the visitor will see the remains of other huts in a field. Sadly this is all that remains of a large settlement that was recorded in the 19th century but destroyed by the farmers plough in the 1870's.

Caesar recorded that it was customary for the European Celts to offer the loot gained in battle to their gods by casting it into lakes or leaving it in sacred groves. It is obvious that Llyn Cerrig Bach, near Valley, is one of these sacred lakes, but it is impossible to say why it was chosen. Perhaps it was the scene of some unique event that became famous, and attracted offerings from many parts of the country.

A magnificent collection of artefacts was found when bulldozers were used to remove the peat from the silted lake so as to compress a new runway at RAF Valley airfield in 1942-3. As the peat was being spread, several of the artefacts caught in the teeth of the harrow. The finds, over a hundred items in all, indicate much military involvement and some, associated with the Roman invasion on the Druids, represent an untypical selection of items. The finds date from around 200 BC to the middle of the first century AD, proving that this was not a casual loss. As they were discovered during wartime, a rather hurried excavation was carried out by Sir Cyril Fox. Many of the objects recovered were associated with warfare, and some had been deliberately bent or broken, perhaps as a dedication to the gods before casting them into the water. It is also impossible to tell if this vast collection of goods were the spoils from local skirmishes or brought to Môn from further afield. If they had been brought from elsewhere, then this would confirm the theory that Môn was considered to be a centre of the Druid religion. The artefacts are now on display at the National Museum of Wales in Cardiff, and provide the visitor with some exceptionally fine examples of swords, spears, shields, horse harnesses, chariot fittings and ornaments. Most notable are the eleven swords and eight spearheads, as well as parts of a magnificent display shield.

Interestingly, the wheels of twenty-two chariots were unearthed, and this may indicate an offering of wheels only, which we know were sacred to one of the gods. However, the large quantity of bones found, including the remains of ox, horse, sheep and pig, may suggest that the lake was also used for sacrificial ceremonies.

One explanation given is that the objects indicate that Môn was once a place of refuge for people from other parts of Britain, and that these were their personal gifts offered to the gods in return for a safe refuge on the island. On the other hand as there appears to be no items later than 60 AD, a date which coincides with the arrival of the Romans, this may well have been the Druid's final attempt to implore the gods for help before the Roman onslaught.

CHAPTER EIGHT

THE DRUIDS AND THE ROMANS

The religious leaders of the Celts were the Druids, the priests who claimed to know the will of the gods with whom they communicated directly. They were the teachers, historians and philosophers who claimed to have expert knowledge in astrology, astronomy, medicine and magic. They were particularly strict on the young people they taught, who had to learn everything by heart. No writing aids were allowed because the Druids placed a religious ban on everything other than the spoken word, for fear of it falling into the wrong hands.

Some historians claim that they were, with the exception of the Greeks and the Romans, the most advanced of all intellectual classes amongst the peoples of ancient Europe. However, the Roman writers of the day viewed the Druids in a different light. They claimed that they were a barbaric race who indulged in human sacrifice, and searched for prophecy in the entrails of their victims.

The word Druid is thought to have been derived from the Greek word Drus, meaning an oak. It has even been suggested that it may have originated as a nickname derived from their sacred oak-woods with which they were associated. However, other historians point out that the favourite tree of the Druids was the rowan, and it was on a frame of interwoven twigs and branches of this tree that the Druids would sleep in order to receive their prophetic visions. However, it is from Pliny, the elder, who came from a family of Roman colonists in Gaul, that we first hear about the oak groves and mistletoe. 'The Druids – so they call their magicians – hold nothing more sacred than the mistletoe and the tree on which it grows provided it is an oak. They choose the oak to form groves, and they do not perform any religious rites without its foliage.'

Pliny himself was extremely interested in magic and it is from him also that we first read of the Druid or serpents eggs, which tradition informs us were produced by the foam of hissing snakes meeting together. The foam formed a ball, which was tossed in the air and, if caught by a Druid, could be used to cancel any magic spell. Pliny claimed that he had seen one of these eggs, which was like a crystal or glass bead, and about the size of a modern day apple.

From Publicius Cornelius Tactitus, whose father-in-law was Julius Agricola, a Governor of Britain, we learn that Môn was a great centre for Druid lore. He noted that all potential Celtic leaders were sent from Europe to be instructed, and that it took twenty years to train to become a Druid. A close second come the Vates, whose training lasted for twelve years. They too claimed to possess the art of prophecy and played a role in ritual sacrifices. It took seven years to train to become a bard whose most important function was to compose poetry in praise of people and celebration.

Sadly, despite the modern day fascination with the Celts, very little of what the Druids actually taught is known, which has lead to much speculation. The only certain fact is that these remote ancestors of present day Irish, Highland Scots and Welsh had to face the best organised invasion to take place on British soil.

By this time, Wales had been divided into four parts, which in later times became the four dioceses of Bangor, Llanelwy (St Asaph), Ty Ddewi (St David's) and Llandaf. In the south and south-east the Iberian nomads had formed tribes called the Silures. To the north dwelt the Ordivices, who were also known as the `Hammermen,' because they swept into battle brandishing their flint-headed hammers. In the west lived the Demaete tribes.

Môn had, for some reason, become the centre for economic, religious and political power, and we can only assume that its unique location, sanwiched between the trade routes of Ireland and East Anglia, played a major role in its existence.

Tacitus, the historian, describes Môn as being heavily populated and a sanctuary for fugitives. Julius Caesar informs us that the Druid religion of Europe was 'thought to have been invented in Britain and from there imported into Gaul.' He goes on to say that those who wished to study it in depth would travel to Britain.

Whilst this independent seat of religious resistance continued so close, Gaul could not be pacified. Therefore it would appear that when the Romans, under the leadership of Suetonius Paulinus, the imperial governor of Britain, set out to invade Môn in 61 AD, the destruction of their religion was their prime target. Tacitus explains that it became necessary 'to attack the island of Môn, which was feeding the native resistance.'

We do not know for certain if Chester was occupied by the Romans at the time of the invasion, nevertheless, we do know that the earliest Roman artefact found there was a lead water pipe from about 79 AD. Perhaps we can assume that Suetonius used Chester as his base? What is known is that he led an extremely organised campaign, and when he arrived at the Menai Straits his army consisted of two legions of around six thousand men, and four thousand mercenaries or soldiers of fortune, plus an additional back-up of infantry and cavalry. The attack was launched at low tide so that the horses could swim across the strait. Flat bottomed boats were used to ferry foot soldiers across the Menai Straits. These were built either on Afon Dyfrdwy (the River Dee) and ferried around the coast, or built at Caernarfon. The Romans appeared to have had some knowledge of the area because we are told, by Tactitus, that they needed to deal with the 'shifting shallows.'

Looking over to the shore of Môn the Romans had their first sight of the defenders, and although they were used to seeing armies lined up ready to attack, they were not prepared for the sight of women. Tactitus gives us a graphic account, which is based on an eye-witness account: 'Standing on the shore was the opposing army, a dense formation of men and weapons. Women in black clothing like that of the Furies ran between the ranks. Wild haired, they brandished torches. Around them, the Druids, lifting their hands towards the sky to make frightening curses, frightened (the Roman) soldiers with this extraordinary sight. And so they (the Romans) stood motionless and vulnerable as if their limbs were paralysed. Then their commander exhorted them and they urged one another not to quake before an army of women and fanatics. They carried the ensigns forward, struck down all resistance, and enveloped them in (the enemy's) fire. After that, a garrison was imposed on the vanquished and their groves destroyed, places of savage superstition. For they considered it their duty to spread its altars with the gore of captives and to communicate with the deities though human enrails.'

The last sentence refers to the primitive custom, which claimed that the Druids were able to forecast the future by looking at the entrails of a chicken.

The armies aim was to totally suppress the religious monks and the soldiers showed no mercy. Everyone who stood in their way was slaughtered, including women and the unarmed Druids who offered no resistance, relying on their gods to save them. The soldiers even took the torches off the women and set them alight. As the blood of those who were hacked to death flowed over Môn, the oak groves were torn down and set alight. Altars were smashed and, as the smoke rose from the funeral pyres piled high with murdered victims, the Roman army sought out those who had tried to hide. It is said that on a quiet night, on the edge of Llyn Carreg Bach, the ghostly figures of hooded monks can be heard in prayer as they flee from the sword brandishing soldiers.

As Môn was being ransacked and defeated Suetonius received news that under their Queen, Boudicca (Buddug), the Iceni and other tribes in the south east of Britain had rebelled. Consequently the troops were sent to defend London. Although Suetonius had not succeeded in destroying the Celts, he had managed to strike a devastating blow to the Druids priesthood and, although it was not entirely destroyed, Môn never re-established itself as the centre of Druidism again.

After the departure of the Romans the island began to recover slowly and although the Twentieth Legion were based at Wroxeter on the Welsh borders, they did not present a threat. However, at the end of the summer of 77 AD an incident took place which triggered another attack that would eventually affect Môn. One day, whilst out on an exercise, a troop of Roman soldiers was ambushed and almost totally destroyed by a tribe of the Ordivices on what is now the road from Colwyn Bay to Mochdre. This event lowered the morale of the Roman Army who feared another Boudiccan revolt. However, it was considered by the Romans and the Hammermen to be too late in the year for a major confrontation. Winter was setting in and the Legions dispersed to their home camps, whilst the Hammermen took to their homesteads in the hills.

About the same time Agricola took over as the Imperial Governor of Britain and, possibly to show his authority, he began to take charge of the situation. He called the troops together and marched straight into the Snowdonian mountains to launch a surprise attack on the Hammermen. It was a bold move, and the Ordovices were not prepared, defences were inadequate, and several hill-forts were destroyed or abandoned. Although many Hammermen were massacred, enough escaped to continue to be a threat to the Roman army.

Agricola did not stop there and, now fully aware of the importance of Môn, he invaded the island. This time Agricola chose his troops carefully. He knew that crossing the Menai Straits would not be easy, so he picked those men who had experience with fords, and those able to swim with arms and horses beside them. The inhabitants of Môn were also aware of what was about to happen, but expected the army to arrive again in a flotilla of boats. As they waited and watched for the fleet they were not prepared for the surprise attack by soldiers sneaking up on foot. Panic and disorder resulted. The Romans took advantage of the situation, inflicting a devastating attack on the natives resulting in defeat and surrender to Argicola. The attack was believed to have been launched from a wooden campaign-camp at Caernarfon, which was later replaced by a stone fort using sandstone from Cheshire and tiles from the Roman factory at Holt.

It is well known that the Romans were impressed by the excellent quality of Britain's pearls, and the fresh water mussel pearls of the Conwy river may have been just one of the reasons for the attack on, and the occupation of, North Wales. Also there was an ample supply of copper on

Y Gogarth (the Great Orme) and Mynydd Parys, and the Romans would have been anxious to keep the ore in their control.

It is said that copper from Môn, lead from north-eastern Wales and gold from the Cothi valley were shipped off to be used by the Roman Empire. Pieces of round copper cakes, bearing official Roman stamps, have been found in hut groups around Môn. These cakes were formed by pouring molten metal into a shallow tray, and are distinctive because each has a smooth upper surface immediately inside the perimeter. This is caused by the rapid cooling of the metal at the point of contact with the solid tray. The most famous cake found was at Aberffraw in 1640, and bears the stamp SOCIO ROMAE. It is counter stamped by the word NATSOL. As yet, neither inscriptions have been interpreted, although it is obviously Roman.

By the third century the Roman Empire was declining and several coastal forts were built in Britain including Caergybi, what is now the town of Caergybi, and the watchtower or signal station on Mynydd Caergybi. This indicates that there was still a need to protect the island from invasion, and no doubt one of the prime targets was the copper mines on Mynydd Parys, which were still of vital importance to the declining Roman Empire.

Caergybi is a three sided enclosure with solid towers at each corner. There is also evidence that a wall projected towards the sea on the north-east side which, at some stage, may have protected a quay, possibly used by a naval fleet. This could also have been used in conjunction with the watchtower recently discovered at Caer-y-tŵr. Its position commanded excellent views over the nearby harbour, and could have been seen when approaching from the west. It may have been used to pass messages to the naval base at Caergybi and, by a series of signal stations, forming a link with Chester. Coins found within the tower suggest that it was used during the 4th century. There is no historical record of the building of this fort, but the Life of St Cybi claims that Maelgwn Gwynedd gave him the land to build a monastery in the 6th century. This could be true as deserted forts were often given to the church. Today the parish church of St Cybi lies within the fort boundaries overlooking the harbour. By the south wall of the fort there is a small chapel known as Eglwys y Bedd, which is believed to cover the grave of St Cybi.

As we have seen in the previous chapter, Caer Leb could also have belonged to the Roman period. It is a low lying enclosure defined by double banks and ditches, though the outer bank has been totally destroyed on the northern and eastern sides. The size of the enclosure, together with its marshy location, has sometimes led to it being interpreted as a medieval moated homestead. Excavations in the last century revealed a third-century brooch and a fourth century coin, indicating that the site was in use in the late Roman period, if not earlier. Traces of stone buildings were also recovered, and the platform visible along the north side yielded a medieval coin. Perhaps further archaeological investigation will reveal more concerning this intriguing monument.

In conclusion, the Romans might have devastated Môn, but they left behind a good administration system, a network of forts, which were connected by thousand of kilometres of new roads. This contributed to the joining of mountainous land in a way Scotland and Ireland were never united, and the existence of so many forts helped to ensure peace. Craftsmen were able to use these roads as were poets and, later, evangelists, which in turn helped in the spread of Christianity in Wales. The Romans also left behind many Latin words which have been incorporated into the Welsh language of today. For example, ffenestr for window, castell for fort, pont for bridge and ffos for ditch. The Romans called the land Britain and the people Britons, although they probably called themselves Brython. Wales and Welsh came later when the Saxons introduced these words, meaning foreigners (in their own land).

In spite of fortified protection by the Roman army, Wales remained open to attack from Ireland, particularly for slave raiding. It is at this time we hear the story of young St Patrick being carried off from his Brython home to a life of slavery in the Ulster mountains. At this time also, large numbers of Irishmen settled in Wales, especially in Môn and north-western Wales.

When the Roman Empire finally collapsed at the end of the fourth century, Britain was left to its own devices and Wales became divided between the Brythonic and the Goidelic (the Irish) tribes, which eventually led to a power struggle between the two races.

CHAPTER NINE

BATTLES WITH THE IRISH, PICTS AND SAXONS

By the beginning of the 5th century most of the Roman legions had left Britain, withdrawn by a leader who was later to become the Emperor Constantine III. The majority of the people who lived in Wales during this time, lived in tribes and shared the land with the Irish who had settled here. But unarmed and unprotected, the tribes soon had to face attacks from many invaders, some from within Wales. Others from outside, including the powerful Saxon Kingdoms of Mercia and Northumbria which threatened the area around the Afon Clwyd.

Very little is known for certain about those long dark days, and even the facts concerning such interesting events as the withdrawal of the Romans, and the beginnings of Christianity are shrouded in legend. However, we do know that, although the Goidelic Celts, who were blood thirsty and barbaric, crossed the sea to live in Ireland, for many centuries they continued to be at war and a constant threat to the Brythonic Celts who had displaced them. Over the years there had been a certain amount of settlement by Irish tribes who had established themselves, with the result that many of the Welsh Kings and princes could claim descent from the Irish chiefs. But not satisfied with smaller settlements, the Irish tried to over-run North Wales, and in spite of the Welsh efforts to drive them back, they seemed set on seizing the whole of Wales for themselves. Much later Gildas, the British monk wrote of the invading Irish who arrived in their skin boats, 'whose hulls might be seen creeping across the glassy surface of the water like so many insects awakened from torpor by the heat of the noonday sun and making with one accord for some familiar haunt.'

As we have already seen, in Anglesey there are several clusters of ruined hut dwellings known as Cytiau'r Gwyddelod (Huts of the Irish), and although we have no evidence it has been claimed that these were occupied by the Irish. However, a more likely explanation is that they became the refuge fortresses of the native Celts during these periods of prolonged unrest and Irish raids.

Eventually the constant Irish attacks became such a problem for the people of Gwynedd that they sent for help from their fellow countrymen in the north of England. According to a tradition which was not written down until the ninth century, a fighting force, led by Cunedda Wledig and his eight sons, Osmael, Rumanus, Dunawd, Ceredig, Aflog, Einion Girth, Dogfael and Edern journeyed to Wales around 400.

Cunedda was a Celtic chieftain, or possibly a Romano-Brythonic prince, who came from Manaw Gododdin, the territory of the Gododdin that covered parts of northern England and southern Scotland. His grandfather was called, Padarn Beisrydd (Padarn of the Red Tunic), which may imply that he held high office under the Romans and had worn the Roman purple. It is also possible that Cunedda was sent for at the request of the Romans before their departure. Taliesin, the bard who lived in the second half of the 6th century, referred to him as ' a chief of lion aspect,' and a man who wore a golden belt. This belt was always worn by the Roman leader of the Britons, which gives us some indication of his importance. For the next nine centuries, many future rulers of Wales, particularly those of Gwynedd, claimed to have descended from Cunedda. They established the most powerful dynasty that the native population was ever to possess – that of the house of Gwynedd at Aberffraw. Although, as we have seen from the story of Branwen that featured in the Mabinogion, the court of Aberffaw possibly dates from a much earlier period, it may well have fallen into disrepair and was re-established again as a Royal Court at this date. We shall read more of the princes of Gwynedd in chapter eleven.

The arrival of Cunedda is a significant event in Welsh history, but it was left to Cunedda's grandson Cadwallon Lawhir, to complete the task by defeating the Irishman Sergei at Cerrig-y-Gwyddyl near Trefdraeth in Anglesey around 470. According to tradition, Cadwallon and his men were so determined to gain control of their land, or else die in the attempt, that they bound their legs together with horses' fetterlocks so that they could not turn and run. Their tactics worked and Sergei was slain. Near the Parish Church at Caergybi (Holyhead) stands a smaller church, Eglwys y Bedd, and it is claimed that the bones of the Irish leader lie buried here, along with St Cybi, as mentioned earlier.

Without this success Wales might well have become another Irish colony. Although this battle subdued the Irish settlers, it is apparent that the Irish influence survived. The name Gwynedd itself is derived from the Irish. Interestingly, the name of Llyn (as in peninsula) is also Irish, and is related to the word Leinster.

The result of this critical battle is partly confirmed in Historia Brittonum written by Nennius, a cleric based at Bangor. In about 800 he wrote, in Latin, a compilation of all the historical and geographical legendary material he could find. In the preface he describes himself as a disciple of Elbodugus (Elfodd), Bishop of Bangor. Nennius was aware that his source material was scarce and wrote. 'since the scholars of the island of Britain had no knowledge, and put no records in books, I have made a heap of what I have found.' He also went on to explain that he worked from the records of the Romans, the church, the Irish, and the English as well as using the oral traditions of story-telling.

In this work he credits Einion Yrith, Cunedda's eldest son, with the defeat of the Irish and the unity of the Welsh in the north-west. It is in this account that we are told that Cunedda was accompanied by his eight sons, and that the campaign of Cunedda against the invading Irish was well planned, but a long drawn out battle.

Nennius was the first to write that the regions of Wales, most notably Meirionnydd, Edeyrnion and Ceredigion, were named after, or to the glory of, the sons of Cunedda. The truth is that these place names were possibly already in place at that time, and it has long been a tradition to attempt an explanation of why an area was given a particular name. As was previously mentioned, Nennius used all sorts of sources for his Historia; most of it was based on legend rather than fact, and he never mentioned his own imagination in the credits. There is not a truly verifiable source relating to the existence of Cunedda himself, let alone his eight sons, and names could easily change from generation to generation as fact became history, and history became legend. What is certain is that Cunedda, real or not, formed a dynasty that would provide Wales with her royal princes for centuries to come.

The Irish weren't the only invaders who proved a problem for the Celts. During Roman times the Teutonic tribes of Northern Germany, the Saxons, were always troublesome. Now left to their own devices they pressed along the eastern coast and between 450 and 600 established settlements in the lower regions of the country.

When the mists of history clear, some hundred years later, we find the nation we now call Welsh already formed. The king who, after the expulsion of the Irish from Anglesey, inherited a new, stable North Wales was Cadwallon's son, Maelgwn Gwynedd. Because of his father's victory over the Irish in Môn he was also known as the Island's Dragon, since the power of his family had been conclusively proved on the island. He had his main seat at Deganwy overlooking Afon Conwy and ruled until 547. He was a man with an abundance of energy, and during his lifetime did a great deal to enforce a sense of unity throughout Wales.

No actual battles were credited to him, although it appears that he did exercise his authority in more direct ways. It is said that he murdered his wife, the sister of Brochwel King of Powys, and also his nephew, so that he could marry his nephew's wife. Other sources claim that he also murdered his uncle so that he could take the crown in the first place, although it does seem more likely that he did inherit Gwynedd and Môn from his father.

We have only one author to guide us through this dark period of history. Gildas, was a fault finding, yet extremely learned British monk, who condemned Maelgwn as the worst of all the bad kings ruling the west at the time. But Gildas could not find any other good kings either! He wrote of Maelgwn Gwynedd as a mighty warrior, but a prince who 'closes his ears to the music of Heaven and listens only to the flattery of the bards.' Gildas, however, did remember with affection the days of Roman rule. About 540 he wrote De Excidio in which he detailed the corrupt and wicked life of five British kings. Here he includes the mysterious figure of Vortigern (Celtic over-lord, who was Gwrtheyrn in Welsh tradition), the traitor ruler who allowed the Saxons into the Celtic lands. He also invited the Jutes of Hengist and Horsa into Britain, to act as mercenaries against the raids of the Saxons. As soon as Hengist and Horsa had arrived, they decided to take over Vortigern's kingdom. Vortigern's son Brydw (or Cadell Ddyrnllug) had quarrelled with his father and was supported by Germanus, Bishop of Auxerre, in becoming ruler of modern Powys. Germanus had helped the British defeat an attack of Saxons and Picts at Maes Garmon, which has been identified as Mold in Flint. He then turned his wrath on Vortigern, pursuing him until he was tracked down in Dyfed, where it is claimed he perished on the banks of the Afon Teifi.

If we can believe legend, and that Vortigern was indeed the High King of Britain and the only person able to unite the British Celts against the invading Saxons, then his death was a tragic blow. Three years after his death a letter was sent to the Roman ruler Aetius in Gaul, appealing for military aid against the invaders. It became known as Gemitus Britannorum – 'The Groans of the British!'

As the 5th century drew to a close, Britain became lost in the mist of continual warfare between the Celts and Anglo-Saxons, and this is the age of those wonderful legends concerning King Arthur and his Knights.

The steady Saxon advance across the whole of Britain was temporarily halted by a British military leader, possibly the legendary King Arthur, at the battle of Mount Badon (Brwydr Mynydd Baddon) around 496. The location of this battle is not known, but according to the Annales Cambriae it was Arthur who succeeded in uniting the Celts against the invaders. However, Arthur was killed at the battle of Camlan, which was supposed to have been fought around 515.

Towards the end of the 6th century, the mists begin to clear and we find that Britain was no longer a Celtic island. The Anglo-Saxons were in firm control of the lowlands – Kent, the South Saxons, the West Saxons, the East Saxons, the East Angles and Mercia, Deira and Bernica in the north. By the year 577 Caewlin and Cutha forced a Saxon wedge between the Celts in the area now known as Wales, and the Celts in the western peninsula Dumnonia, now Devon and Cornwall. The northern Celts (in northern England and Scotland) were also isolated. To the invading Saxons, the Celts were merely foreigners weahlas or welisc, hence the modern name of Wales and Kern-welisc for Cornwall.

CHAPTER TEN

CHRISTIANITY AND SAINTLY TALES

Christianity came to Wales long before the inhabitants of England were converted by the mission of St Augustine in Kent in the 590's, and even then it was only a limited conversion. It appears that the Celts of Gaul were certainly amongst the first to accept Christianity from Rome, and it also seems logical that the Celts in Britain learnt of the new religion from them.

Legends concerning the arrival of Christianity among the Island Celts are numerous. One claims that Bran the Blessed brought the faith to the island in the middle of the 1st century AD. Another name closely associated with Celtic Christianity is Elen, the Brythonic born wife of Magnus Maximus (Macsen Wledig of Welsh tradition) who was declared Emperor by his legions in 383. Magnus was an ambitious man and was not content with being just the 'Western Emperor'. In 387 he marched his legions into Italy, and by January of the following year Rome was within his grasp. According to Ammianus Marcellinus, the emperor was recognised in battle by his imperial standard showing a dragon on a purple flag, believed by some to be the origin of the red dragon of Wales.

After her husband's death, Elen is said to have taken her large family back to Britain where she began to work on behalf of the Christian movement in Wales. She gave her name to Capel Elen in Penrhosllugwy and several other church foundations around Wales.

St Tysilio's church, which rests on land tucked neatly under Pont y Borth (the Menai Bridge), is said to have been the place where Christianity was first preached in Môn. In those days the site was an island. Tysilio was the son of Brochwel, King of Powys, and his mother was Arddun, daughter of Pabo Post Prydain. He was the first cousin of St Asaph and St Deiniol, and lived in Shewsbury. From a young age he aspired to become a religious leader, but his father wanted him to take up arms and fight for his country. Tysilio was a head-strong young man, and one day whilst out hunting with his brothers, decided to run away. He went to Meifod on the junction of Afon Einion and Afon Fyrnwy and threw himself at the feet of Abbot Gwyddfarch, who lived there. Meanwhile his brothers returned home and told their father what had happened. Brochwel ordered a company of men to go to Meifod to bring his son back. They accused the Abbot of influencing the lad, but when Tysilio appeared shaven and habited as a monk he persuaded them that this was his decision. Fearing that his father would make further trouble,

Tysilio asked if he could go to a remote spot, and he was sent to the island in the Menai Straits. He spent seven years there before returning to Meifod where he discovered that Gwyddfarch was planning on taking a trip to Rome. Tysilio knew that the abbot was too old to take such a journey and offered to go in his place. The Abbot refused, so Tysilio took him on a long mountain journey. When he was too exhausted to go any further, Tysilio allowed him to lie down and rest. When he finally woke Tysilio asked him how he could think of going on such a long journey to Rome when a short mountain journey had tired him. The abbot told him that he had had a dream, and in this dream he had dreamt of seeing a magnificent city before he died. Tysilio realised that he should not stop him, and allowed him to go to Rome. Not long after his return Gwyddfarch died, and Tysilio succeeded him as abbot. St Tysilio is credited as having written a history of the Brythoniaid which, after it had been taken to Normandy, Armorica and then back to Wales, was lost.

Maelgwn Gwynedd is closely connected with the coming of Christianity to Wales. Gildas claimed that Maelgwn was educated by 'the most refined master of almost all Britain.' Later scholars claim that both were taught by St Illtud, the founder of a monastery in South Wales in the early sixth century.

Maelgwn is also recorded as being a Christian benefactor by granting land to many monasteries. One example is the Roman fort at Caergybi (Holyhead) which he gave to St Cybi in 540, a possible explanation why the parish Church now stands in the middle of the Roman enclosure.

At this time too, another of Anglesey's famous saints, St Seiriol, set up his church on the opposite side of the island at Penmon or on the nearby island, known as Ynys Seiriol (Puffin Island), also an area where Maelgwn is said to have shown a great interest. St Seiriol was the brother of Einion Frenin, a cousin of Maelgwn. It is reputed that he received the island from his brother, who had also established a religious community on Ynys Enlli (Bardsey Island). The well in which St Seiriol baptised his converts, can still be seen. The healing powers of the well attracted many sick and infirmed people during the eighteenth century, and the upper part of the chamber had to be rebuilt at this time. Today coinage is thrown into the well in the hope that it will bring good luck to the person throwing the gift. Attached to the cell, and in front of the well, was a small building in which the inhabitants of the island assembled for prayer and instruction. Penmon became an important mother church, or clas, with the power of ecclesiastical authority over much of the area.

Situated close to the cell and the well is the later Augustinian Priory. It is almost certain that Gruffudd ap Cynan, or his son, provided the capital for the earliest church of St Seiriol sometime in the 11th or early 12th century. Then around 1220-40 the church was converted to a priory because the Princes of Gwynedd and Powys were supporters of the Augustinian House at Haughmond in Shropshire, and by the 13th century had encouraged the transformation of the most distinguished churches in north Wales to houses for the Augustinian cannons. The building, now in ruins, consisted of three storeys. The ground floor served as a cellar with the dining room above, and the dormitories on the top floor. During meal times, silence was strictly observed by the monks whilst one of them, seated at a window, read aloud. The seat used is by the window in the south-east corner of the building. At this eastern end of the building is a small two storey block, which was added in the 16th century. This may have been used as a 'warming house' or perhaps a private apartment with a kitchen above. The Priors house was probably in the west end of the cloister, but this has been extensively altered and is now a private dwelling.

There is an interesting legend concerning St Seiriol and St Cybi, who were said to be good friends. St Cybi was always sunburned and it is claimed that this was because the two saints would always meet at Llanerchymedd, in the centre of the island. Every morning St Cybi would set out from Holyhead and the sun would be on his face. Late in the day, after his meeting with St Seiriol he would journey back to Holyhead. This time the sun would again be in his face, and so he acquired a tan. Conversely, St Seiriol had the sun on his back in both directions and therefore remained pale, which accounts for why they became known as Cybi the Tawny and Seiriol the Fair.

In the Middle Ages it was the practice of monks to carry images of the saints to exchange for food and other products. For example, an image of St Seiriol together with nine cheeses may have been exchanged for some wool or flour. As well as acting as currency these images were also believed to bring the farmers prosperity, and were therefore very popular.

Wales is fortunate in having many stones to commemorate the lives of Christians who died long before Augustine brought Christianity to England. The rarest are those that bear, in addition to the Latin inscription, the Chi-Rho symbol. This was a monogram formed from the two initial letters (X – the Chi) and P (rho) of the name of Christ, written in Greek. Two of these can be seen in North Wales – one at Treflys and the other at Penmachno. None, as yet, have been found in Môn (Anglesey).

However, many simple stones featuring crosses of varying types and including inscriptions prefixed by Hic Iacit have been found. These often gave details of the dead person's father, and one such stone can be seen in the chancel of Penrhos Llugwy church which is located on high ground to the south of a minor road off the A5025 a little north of Llanallgo. The church is locked and, sadly, there is no indication where a visitor can obtain a key. However, the visitor can see the stone and the inscription clearly through the north window. It is thought to date from the middle of the sixth century, some hundred years before Pope Gregory sent Augustine on his mission to Kent. The stone bears the simple inscription Cundeus Hic Iacit and is believed to commemorate the death of a Christian Irish Chief. Interestingly, there are several Irish memorial stones in Anglesey, which again proves that the Irish did settle and live harmoniously with the people of the island.

Two miles east of the village of Aberffraw, where Llangadwaladr now stands, is what was once the royal burial ground for members of the family of Cunedda, who ruled Môn and Gwynedd for many centuries. One of the royal memorials still survives and is the most important gravestone in Môn. It was found close to the church and, before 19th century restoration work, was used as a lintel above the south door The stone bears the inscription: Catmanus Rex Sapientisimus Opiniatisimus Omnium Regum (Catamanus wisest and most famous of all kings). Catamanus is the Latinised form of Cadfan who claimed direct descendency from Cunedda. This inscription is very interesting, because it shows a typical example of early inscriptions which ignores spacing and leaves words ending on the next line. The original lettering is interesting too. The N's are written like H's, and the U's have a squared bottom, which makes it contemporary with the period of the king. The stone was erected in 625 by his grandson, Cadwaladr, who was to give his name to the village and his patronage to the church. Nothing survives of the church of Cadfan's day, but it is more than likely that it would have been a wooden building. Today the stone is set into the north wall opposite the door, allowing visitors the privilege of seeing one of the most remarkable Christian memorial stones in Britain.

However, don't ignore the rest of the present church, which has some of the best church architecture to be seen in Anglesey. The south transept, built in 1661, by Anne, widow of Col Hugh Owen of Bodewen, is an excellent example of the late Gothic period. The east window in the chancel contains the only medieval glass to survive in any quantity in Anglesey. Do also look at the 19th century gargoyles!

Another Christian memorial stone not to miss is tucked away on the south eastern corner of the island at Llansadwrn, north of Porthaethwy (Menai Bridge). The stone was dug up in the churchyard and is now on the north side of the church. It is considered to be the oldest in Môn, dating from around 530. It commemorates Sadwrn, who was the brother of St Illtud. The inscription reads: Saturninus se(pultus) (I) acit et sua sa(ncta) coniu(n)x. Pa(x) vobiscum sit (Satirninus (which is the Latin form of Sadwrn), and his saintly wife lie buried here. Peace be with you both.) Again the church is kept locked, sadly a reflection of the times we live in, but the key may be obtained from the nearby farmhouse.

After the arrival of the Normans, the native Celtic communities continued to serve the churches throughout the twelfth century, together with the patronage of the Princes of Wales.

Further evidence of early Christianity can be found all around Ynys Môn and one area not to be missed is Ynys Llanddwyn, associated with St Dwynwen (patron saint of Welsh lovers). To call Llanddwyn an island is a misnomer as it is really a peninsula that divides Llanddwyn bay from the breakers of Malltraeth Bay. It may be reached from (Niwbwrch) Newborough, south-west of Llanfair Pwllgwyngyll on the A4080 where you need to take the road for Pen-Lôn. Here you can park the car and walk south-west along the edge of Newborough warren. Turn right along the beach and follow the sign-posted footpath for Landline Island. This will lead you through grassy hillocks and rocky coves, with some fantastic views of Snowdonia in the distance. The island is now part of the National Nature Reserve and is home to an array of wild flowers and cormorants. Ancient breeds of sheep also graze in an enclosure.

St Dwynwen was one of the twenty-four beautiful daughters of Brychan, a fifth century Welsh prince of Brycheiniog (Brecon). Interestingly nearly all his children ended up as 'Saints'. Legend informs us that, after an unhappy love affair, Dwynwen sought solitude on the island. She was so anxious that others should not suffer a similar fate, that she gave the waters of a little well close to her chapel miraculous powers which would enable future lovers to determine their faithfulness, as well as the faithfulness of their partners. This was achieved by a ritual, called the divination of the fishes. First a few crumbs of freshly baked bread was sprinkled on the water, then a handkerchief was spread on the water. A sacred eel would appear from the depths of the well, and if the handkerchief was disturbed in anyway, the faithfulness of the lover was confirmed. Offerings would then be placed at the shrine of the Saint. Today the well is often choked with seaweed, but it is claimed that an eel still lives there, and any anxious lovers can make a pilgrimage to the well. St Dwynwen's 's Day is observed on 25 January, and naturally after her death, in 465, her chapel became a popular place of pilgrimage. Between the well and the chapel the visitor can see a small but prominent rock with a cleft that looks as though the rock has been split by an axe. It is claimed that when St Dwynwen was dying she asked to be carried outside so that she could see the glorious sunset, which incidentally is something not to be missed. She was placed in a shelter in the rock, which immediately spilt apart so that she could have a clearer view of the setting sun.

Today very little remains of St Dwynwen's church. The walls, the chancel and the arches to the east are still visible, and it is possible to trace the rest of the building in the form of a small cross from the markings on the ground. Human remains have been discovered both inside the church and in a small field beyond. To commemorate those buried here there is a modern Celtic cross bearing the inscription:

'They lie around did living tread
This sacred ground, now silent, dead.'

Another cross in commemoration of St Dwynwen, bearing the date 25 January 465, was erected in 1897 and stands on the headland, looking out to sea.

Another interesting church to visit is at the north end of Llangaffo, a little north-west of Niwbwrch, on the B4419. At first glance this 19th century church looks like any other ridge top village church, and will give the observer no indication of the importance of the site in the early middle ages, or the wealth of artefacts which survive today. The key can be obtained from a cottage at the entrance to the graveyard.

The church at Llangaffo is dedicated to St Gaffo, a friend of St Cybi, and it is likely that a monastery existed here from an early date. The earliest stone in the collection dates from the 7th century and was found at Fron Deg, about eight hundred metres to the south. The stone is to be found at the church in the room where sacred vessels are kept. The inscription, written horizontally, reads: Govern (perhaps an early form of Gwern), son of Cuuris Cini, set up his stone. The wording suggests that this is not a gravestone but a commemorative memorial. It was quite a common feature, later on, to erect crosses in commemoration of some great event, and the exceptional feature of Llangaffo is the number of cross-inscribed stones that have survived. The broken head of one such cross lies by the entrance door. It was a wheel-cross, cut from one single piece of stone. When complete it would have looked like the stones at Penmon, and would probably have stood at the entrance to a monastic enclosure. This site could well have been equal in importance to that of Penmon in the 10th century. Five stones stand against a low wall opposite the church door, and two pieces of another have been built into the graveyard wall, facing the road. The largest stone amongst the group dates from the 12-13th century, whilst others belong to the 9-11th centuries.

The church of St Eilian has a sinister warning for any visitor. The rood screen features a skeleton and the text Colyn angau yw pechod (sin is the sting of death)! The church may be reached along the winding lanes that lead from the village of Amlwch to the north-east of the A5025. It is one of the most interesting churches in the area. In the churchyard, to the south east of the church, stands St Eilian's chapel, which is traditionally said to occupy the site of his original cell in the fifth century. Amongst the rocks, about half a mile from the church, sits a sacred well, Ffynnon Eilian. The well is not easy to find, and today it is dry; but it was once renown for its powers in curing agues, fits and scrofula. On St Eilian's Eve (13 January), people would visit the well and sip its waters, before kneeling and praying. Afterwards they would place offerings, usually groat pieces, in a chest known as Cyff Eilian. Don't miss seeing the cyff which is still in the church, on the west wall, and dated 1667.

Also preserved in the church are a pair of dog-tongs, a relic of the days when people took their dogs to church. Apparently there were no objections to the presence of the dogs in the church, but the tongs were used to throw out those who decided to fight during the service! It has also been claimed that Communion rails were first erected, by the order of Archbishop Laud, to prevent the dogs from fouling the altars! In the chapel, separate from the church, was a little wooden shrine – something like a small witness box. Tradition relates that if you could squeeze into it, and turn around three times, you would be cured of all diseases, and could expect to add a further five years on to your life. Sadly, this shrine has now disappeared, perhaps due to overuse?

Before leaving the vicinity, don't miss the stone pillar in the churchyard which, according to some historians, was once a preaching cross.

CHAPTER ELEVEN

THE PRINCES OF GWYNEDD

As we have already discovered the princes of Gwynedd began around 400 with Cunedda whose influence was so great that his leadership continued with his sons and grand-sons. One hundred and forty-six years later his great grandson, Maelgwn Gwynedd, was as powerful as Cunedda had ever been. At the mouth of Afon Dyfi there is a wide sandy estuary, over which the tides flow. Part of this is called Traeth Maelgwn, and there is a romantic legend associated with Maelgwn. It is claimed that it was here that all the chiefs had assembled to choose their gwledig or pendragon, (chief dragon), the leader of all leaders who would wear the dragon as his ensign. The title would go to the one able to remain seated the longest as the tide came in. Everyone had gathered to witness this great event. It is said that one of Maelgwn's advisors had made him a chair of waxed birds' wings. When the tide came in, all the other princes were driven away and only Maelgwn remained, floating triumphantly on his chair, to became the over-lord of them all.

We learn from Gildas that most of Maelgwn's youth was spent in war and violence, so it is not surprising that he became an able military leader. It is claimed that in the early years of his youth he also overthrew his maternal uncle, although his name is unknown to us. Not long after this he gave up his royal status to become a monk, but soon found monastic life unbearable and returned home.

Although we know very little about the period from 400 to 546 we do know from Gildas that Roman towns were being abandoned and the country suffered a great famine. In 446 someone, and we are not certain who, sent a letter to Consul Aëlius, commander of the Western Empire begging for help, but the letter went unheeded. It is clear from the writings of Gildas that he blames Vortigern for the downfall of the country, but the fact that there were many ruling kings did not help matters. Britain was not ruled by one high-king and whilst some courts were only just surviving, others like Maelgwn's seat at Deganwy, were wallowing in luxury by Dark Age standards.

Gildas's writing is contemporary with the times, and it is evident that he hoped Maelgwn would read what he had to say about him. 'Why wallow like a fool in the ancient ink of your crimes, like a man drunk on wine pressed from the vines of Sodom,' he writes. We may well query why the ruler of a small kingdom was able to afford to import wine from the Mediterranean, but archaeologists have proved this fact by finding shards of imported wine jars at the Deganwy site. Gildas also blames the low moral standards and the evil deeds of its leaders for the downfall of the country. He details faults one by one. He clearly knows Maelgwn personally and states that he has leading qualities which, if he had not been corrupted, would have led to his success. 'You are last on my list,' he writes, 'but first in evil, stronger than many at once in power and wickedness, abundant in giving, profuse in sin, strong in arms, but stronger in the destruction of the soul, oh Maglocunus.' The evil deed may refer to the murders outlined in chapter nine. However, Gildas also claims that Maelgwn's position and tall stature set him apart from the rest of the kings, thus demonstrating respect for the man. Clearly Gildas was a man of mixed emotions as far as Maelgwn was concerned.

Many other stories are told of Maelgwn and it seems we have a distorted view of the man. He was very interested in poetry and music and surrounded himself with bards. He was a Christian, and helped in the founding of several monasteries, but he did have a short temper and certainly did not suffer fools gladly.

Maelgwn had hoped to die a hero in battle but instead died of the yellow plague, an epidemic which spread across Europe in the middle of the 6th century. The Welsh annals record the year 547 as an 'anno mortalitas magna', a year of great death. Thousands died, and so great was the fear of the people that many took to boats and fled to Brittany. Once again we have been provided with a legend relating to his death. The story tells how the poet-prophet Taliesin foretold the death of the king by a great yellow monster. In his fear Maelgwn locked himself in the church of Llanrhos near Llandudno. One day looking out of the keyhole he saw a yellow monster approaching the church and, it is said, the mere sight of the monster killed him. More than likely he was already infected by the plague when he entered the church and would have died anyway.

Maelgwn was succeeded by his son Rhun, and it seems there is only one historical event connected with him. When Clydno Eiddin and Rhydderch Hael returned to the north after attacking Arfon in revenge for the death of Elidyr, Rhun is said to have retaliated by leading an army as far as the river Forth. When Rhun died he was succeeded by his son Beli, and almost nothing is known of him.

By 577 Urien of Rheged had beaten the Northumbrians into the sea, having besieged the enemy on the island of Lindisfarne. In so doing he met his death when he was betrayed by one of his followers, who murdered him out of jealousy. The Angles took advantage of the situation and seized further territory, and an attempt by the kingdom of Gododdin to recover from this ended in a further defeat. Around 600 the king of

Gododdin assembled his force for an attack on the town of Catraeth, modern day Catterick, which was the point of time when Deira and Bernica joined together with Northumbia. The exercise ended in failure and there was no stopping the new enlarged Northumbria.

The Welsh bard Aneirin lived in the kingdom of Gododdin, and served at the court in Edinburgh. He wrote an elegy in honour of the men who were killed in battle with the Angles at Catterick. It began:

The men who went to Catterick were thirsty for war
The best mead in their honour might have as well been poison
Three hundred ordered out against the army
And for all the celebration, silence
And for all the churcing the priests
Death their last reward.

When the two kingdoms of Bernica (an area in the eastern borders of England and Scotland) and Deira (from the Humber north to Cleveland) amalgamated, Edwin, the heir of Deira, was still a baby, and was hurriedly placed in exile. Cadfan, the son of Iago ap Beli, was now king of Gwynedd and he gave him refuge at his court in Aberffraw, Here in safety the young Edwin was brought up with Cadfan's son Cadwallon. Some historians relate tales of the two princes racing their horses along the beach at Aberffraw, bonded by a kind of 'brotherly' love. He remained here until he grew up and moved east to Cheshire where he married Ceorl, daughter of the king. Nothing much is known of Cadfan's history beyond the fact that he ruled Gwynedd, although the inscription on the stone in the church of Llangadwaladr, that was mentioned in the previous chapter, suggests that he was better than all the other kings. Who knows? Perhaps this meant that his kingdom was rated supreme amongst the others in Wales.

Ethelfrith, who was now the king of Northumbria, was alarmed at the prospect of an allegiance forming between the Deirans and the Welsh, and decided to go into battle with the Welsh. By 613 the Northumbrians had travelled as far south as Powys. We are not absolutely sure where a battle took place, but it is probable that the site was on the river Dee, near Bangor Is-coed, because Bede tells us that,

'the monks of the monastery of Dunawd poured forth, after a fast of three days, and, ascending the hill that commanded the field, prayedfor victory and cursed the enemy.'
Ethelfrith seeing the monks gave the order for his men to massacre them.

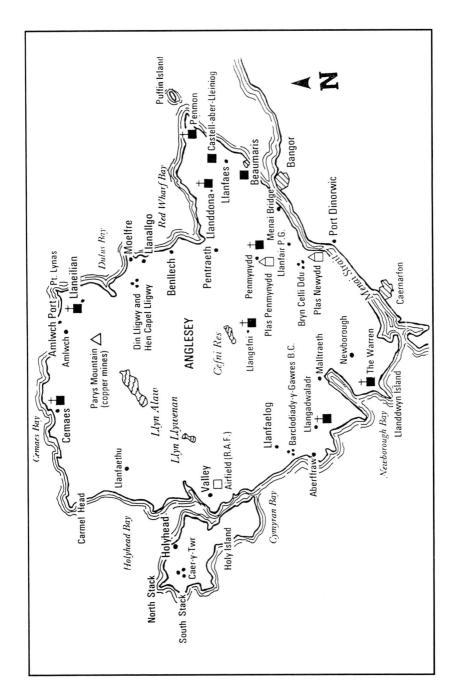

N

Puffin Island

Penmon

Castell-aber-Lleiniog

Beaumaris

Bangor

Llanfaes

Llanddona

Llanallgo

Moelfre

Red Wharf Bay

Menai Bridge

Llanfair P.G.

Port Dinorwic

Dulas Bay

Benllech

Pentraeth

Penmynydd

Plas Penmynydd

Bryn Celli Ddu

Plas Newydd

Din Lligwy and
Hen Capel Lligwy

ANGLESEY

Cefni Res

Llangefni

Pt. Lynas

Llaneilian

Amlwch Port

Amlwch

Parys Mountain
(copper mines)

Menai Strait

Caernarfon

Newborough

The Warren

Llanddwyn Island

Llyn Alaw

Llyn Llywenan

Cemaes

Cemaes Bay

Llanfaethu

Carmel Head

Holyhead Bay

Airfield (R.A.F.)

Valley

Llanfaelog

Barclodiady-y-Gawres B.C.

Llangadwaladr

Malltraeth

Aberffraw

Cymyran Bay

Newborough Bay

Holyhead

Caer-y-Twr

Holy Island

North Stack

South Stack

65

Menai Suspension Bridge and Church Island

Looking down the straits towards Britannia Bridge

The old toll-house on the suspension bridge

One of the lions on Britannia Bridge

The Marquis of Anglesey Column, near Llanfair Pwllgwyngyll

Melin Llynon

Penmon Priory

Ynys Seiriol (Puffin Island) *and Penmon*

The old monastery tower on Ynys Seiriol

Beaumaris castle before it was restored

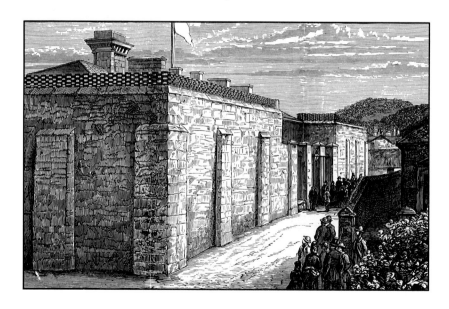

Anglesey County Gaol, Beaumaris

The balance and beauty of Beaumaris castle is shown clearly in this aerial photograph

Siwan, the princess of Wales' coffin

Ynys Llanddwyn

Lligwy cromlech

Moelfre

Benllech

Joseph Rodgers, seaman of the Royal Charter

Llanbadrig church, Amlwch

Llanlliana, Amlwch

St Cwyfan's church, Aberffraw

The harbour, Cemaes

South Stack lighthouse

The Irish Mail Boats, Holyhead

Twelve hundred monks were murdered in cold blood, their prayers still on their lips and their empty hands uplifted to heaven. Only fifty managed to escape before the battle between the two armies commenced.

The Battle of Chester held considerable significance for Wales. The wars between the English and the Welsh had begun. From now on, Wales as a nation had to defend itself almost continuously against attacks from various kings of England. Concerning this battle, we have two conflicting accounts of what really happened. Bede, in the Anglo-Saxon Chronicles, who incidentally manages to get the date wrong, says,

'This year (607) Ethelfrith led his army to Chester, where he slew an innumerable host of the Welsh . . . There were also slain two hundred priests, who came hither to pray for the army of the Welsh . . . Their leader was called Selyf ap Cynan, who with some fifty men escaped thence.'

Geoffrey of Monmouth, on the other hand gives a different account.

'A tremendous fight took place at Bangor, in which many fell on both sides, and Ethelfrith was wounded and put to flight, after losing ten thousand and sixty-six men.'

Around 625 Cadwallon succeeded his father as king of Gwynedd, and thanks to the part he played in English affairs, as told by Bede, we have a good record of Cadwallon's activities. The most significant event was that the Northumbrian king had been killed, and Edwin had been made their king. Then for some unexplained reason he turned on his former allies, namely his foster brother Cadwallon's kingdom.

In the 630's Cadwallon's was forced to retreat, first to the Isle of Anglesey, then to Ynys Seiriol where he was besieged for a while, and finally fled to Ireland. This was not an acceptable situation for the Welsh, or the other Anglo-Saxon kingdoms, and it was to Mercia, a natural ally of Gwynedd, that Cadwallon finally turned for help.

If Edwin was to keep his Saxon rivals at bay, he needed the help of Mercia too, but Mercia now had a new king, Penda, who had reason to fear Edwin's power. When Cadwallon came out of exile and approached him in 633, he formed an anti-Edwin coalition between Gwynedd and Mercia. The two kings led an army against him and on 14 October 633, Edwin and his son were killed in battle at Doncaster. The victory placed Northumbria in the hands of the two kings who, for a year, ravaged Northumbria with no regard for women or children. Cadwallon was a nominal Christian, who had the ancient and well respected blood of the House of Gwynedd running through his veins. Penda, on the other hand, was a pagan who worshipped Germanic gods, but appeared by the accounts of Bede to be more humane and compassionate than Cadwallon. Bede was writing a history for the church, but from an Anglo-Saxon point of view, and was faced with two very different people. How could he write truthfully and not offend? He accepted the fact that Penda was a pagan, and blamed Cadwallon because he should have respected his religion. He wrote, 'He who called himself a Christian is more savage than any pagan. He is barbarous in temperament and behaviour.'

Suddenly, from nowhere appeared Oswald, who became king of Northumbria. He was the youngest son of Ethelfrith, who during the reign of Edwin had been forced into exile in Scotland. His brothers had been killed during the year by Cadwallon, so it was he who made a claim to the throne. Bede's dilemma was resolved. Oswald was an Angle, a good Christian and a man that he portrayed of great compassion. Oswald pursued the much feared Cadwallon to the north, where eventually he caught up with him at Heavenfield (Hexham in the Tyne valley) and personally killed him.

After the death of Cadwallon, Gwynedd fell under the power of Cadafael ap Cynfedw whose rule ended in 654 with a retreat from the battlefield of Winwead Field. Cadwalader ap Cadwallon then took over, although his reign was uneventful. He is a figure of later bardic lore, and it is claimed in the prophecies of Myrddin (Merlin), the wizard, that Cadwalader would make a treaty with Scotland and return to lead a victory over the Saxons. Much later Henry VII was proud to claim descent from Cadwalader in the 'twenty-second degree,' and the red dragon of Cadwalader was one of the three standards offered when he was crowned king of England in 1485. Cadwalader also appears as Cadwalader the blessed, the patron saint of Llangadwalader in Môn. In the pedigrees of Saints he is also said to be the son of Iago ap Beli, and it is possible that two members of the same family have been confused, especially as so many have the same name.

The men who followed Cadwalader were of less importance and their rule could hardly have extended beyond Môn itself. Cadwalader's grandson, Rhodri Molwynog, died in 754, and he was succeeded by his son, Hywel, who died in 825. This effectively ended the male line of direct descendants from Maelgwn Gwynedd. However, on his uncle's death, Marfyn Frych, the son of Gwriad (who was probably a Manx Chieftain), became king of Môn. The claim had passed to him through Hywel's niece. He later married Nest, the daughter of Cadell ap Brochwel of Powys, and it was their son, Rhodri Mawr who was to spend much of his life fighting off the Danes as we shall see in the next chapter.

Today there is nothing to see of the royal court at Aberffraw, and it is hard to imagine that this little village, with its cluster of cottages and unhurried appearance, was once the centre of administration for the kings and princes of Gwynedd. The excellent sculpture 'The Princes' by Jonah Jones, built in Aberffraw, has little significance unless you have some background information. The site of the palace, a little outside the village, is now a field distinguished only by a low bank near the brow of a slope. If the visitor spends a little time to take in the view and allow the eyes to follow the tidal inlet out across Caernarfon bay, perhaps then the importance of the place will became apparent.

CHAPTER TWELVE

NORSE AND OTHER RAIDS

During the closing years of the 8th century Wales was to face further raids, this time by the Danes. From about 835 onwards they became a serious threat especially to the inhabitants of Ynys Seiriol.

The aim of the early Viking raids was to plunder, but their ever threatening presence is remembered in the survival of Norse names such as Osmund's Eyre (now know as the Gallows) near Beaumaris, and the dangerous rocky islets known as the Skerries off the coast of Môn's north-west corner. The word sker comes from the Norwegian meaning a rock on land or at sea. But it was not until the second half of the 9th century that the Vikings attempted to settle.

The Danes settled in the Isle of Man, Dublin and Limerick, and it was from these well positioned bases that they organized their raids on Môn in 853, 877 and again in 902. These later Vikings re-named Ynys Seiriol, Priestholm, the Priest's island.

Rhodri Mawr succeeded to the throne in 844 and his rule soon spread over the whole of North Wales and much of the south. As we have seen in the previous chapter he inherited his seat at Aberffraw from his grandmother's line, as all the direct male line had died out. The kingdom of Powys came to him on the death of his uncle and, as he had married into the royal house of Ceredigion, part of south Wales came to him on the death of his brother-in-law. In effect he founded two royal lines – through Gruffudd ap Cynan leading to Llewelyn Fawr (the Great), and through his grandson Hywel Dda, leading in due course to the house of Tudor.

During his reign, 844-877, Rhodri Mawr had to cope with many invasions, especially from the Vikings. Evidence shows that he proved to be a bold and vigorous leader and his powerful position prevented the Norsemen from making any impression on Wales. He was also the first leader to unite Wales, and set a pattern for the future. This was probably due of the continuing battles and the need for unity to keep the Vikings out. He was hailed Rhodri Mawr – Rhodri the Great, a distinction that had only been bestowed on two other rulers in the same century – Charles the Great or Charlemange and Alfred the Great.

In 853-854 the Norsemen devastated Môn. This was the first of a long series of raids on the island, which eventually gave the island its Norse name of Ongulsey, after a Norseman called Ongul. In 856 Rhodri defeated another Danish invasion and killed its leader Horm. It was Rhodri's victory over Horm which brought about his international fame, much to the delight of the Irish and the Franks. This success was noted by the Ulster Chronicle and by Sediluis Scottus, an Irish scholar at the court of Emperor Charles the Bold at Liege.

But Rhodri's success was short lived. In 876 he was defeated by the Norsemen at a battle which took place in Môn, on a Sunday – hence its reference in the Chronicles as gweith duw sul. He was forced to seek refuge in Ireland before he and his son, Gwriad, met their deaths at the hands of the Saxons nearly two years later.

After Rhodri's death Wales was divided between his two sons. Anarawd ap Rhodri ruled Môn, and was most probably the victor of the battle on the banks of Afon Conwy in 881. The Welsh regarded this success as God's vengeance for killing Rhodri. At first Anarawd tried to alleviate further attacks by forming an alliance with the Danish kingdom set up at York. This gave the Danes of York the chance to communicate with their kinsmen across the sea in Dublin. However, this friendship was not to last, and Anarawd had to turn for help to King Alfred, who was the acknowledged protector against the Vikings. This protection was desperately needed because, for some reason the raids intensified between 878-918.

In 903, following the capture, by the Irish, of the Norse fortress at Dublin, a band of Norsemen led by Igmunt or Ingimund landed on Môn. There they remained as a source of constant trouble for many years. In 918 Môn was again raided by 'the men of Dublin.'

From some unknown reason between 918 and 952 Wales enjoyed a respite from the Norse raids, and we can only assume that they had turned their attentions to other lands. By now Hywel Dda (the Good), the grandson of Rhodri Mawr, had succeeded to the throne, and it may have been that, by now, the country was strong enough to keep the invaders at bay. It is also possible that England and Wales may have joined together to resist a common enemy, and proven to be too great a force for the invaders.

Hywel Dda is remembered as the king who codified or catalogued the laws of the Celts into an organized form. This was a major development in medieval Wales as it created one of the most advanced legal systems in Europe, and was revised and added to until the 13th century. As the king of South Wales, Hywel had inherited the condition of bondage to the English crown, and it appears that he accepted this situation with protest. He had always admired Alfred the Great. However, when Idwal Foel, King of Gwynedd rebelled against the English and was killed, Hywel attacked Idwal's sons and took the kingdom from them. At the same time, Powys came into his possession as well as the old kingdom of Rhwng

Gwy a Hafren (which later became Radnorshire). As Dyfed already belonged to Hywel he was now ruler over a larger domain than Rhodri Mawr. However, on his death in 950 after a reign of forty years, the sons of Idwal Foel struck out and regained the lordship of Gwynedd and Powys.

It is reported that in 952 'pagans', who were probably the Norsemen, attacked the coast of Môn from their base in Dublin. Over the next nine years frequent attacks continued until in 961 the sons of a Viking, called Abloec, ravaged the monasteries at Holyhead and desecrated many of the churches. Penmon came under severe attack in 961 and again in 971, as did the royal seat at Aberffraw in 968.

As we have seen, the religious settlements were founded in the 6th century, and in the early days there was a college for monks on Ynys Seiriol. In 962 Edgar, who had succeeded Alfred the Great as King of the Saxons in 959, came to North Wales with the purpose of forming a settlement in Môn. It is interesting that an account of this event recalls that:

'Edgar proceeded to North Wales, and summoned to him Iago, son of Idwal, and instead to tribute, which was in accordance of an old law, he exacted on him three hundred wolves' heads yearly, allowing him the liberty of killing them whenever he might, in all the isle of Britain. Then there was peace in North Wales; and that tax was paid in North Wales for five hundred and forty years, that is, as long as any wolf could be found in all the British Isles. After that the English King changed the tribute into gold and silver and cattle as of old.

In 968 Macht-ab-Harold came to Anglesey and devastated Penmon which before was the fairest spot in all the Isle of Mona. And immediately after that came Gotffrid-ab-Harold against Anglesey, and laid it waste, and Edgar gave permission to Goffrid's men to abide in Anglesey, and these united themselves into one tyranny with the men of Edwin; and they never departed thence, nor ever after that could treachery be eradicated from the island,'

Further raids were made on the island of Anglesey in 972, 980, and 987. We also know that a set of fine crosses that had been set up at the gates of St. Seiriol monastery were destroyed during these raids. It is possible that about the year 1000, a high cross was set up in Deer Park at Penmon to replace those destroyed by the Vikings. The cross is large and still has its original base, and the top is made from a separate piece of stone. The decorative pattern is very complex and includes a panel of figures in the manner of the Irish crosses and fulfilled a teaching role. Unfortunately time and weathering makes it difficult to see, but photographs taken earlier show a figure between two standing beasts, who whisper in his ears, this depicts the Temptation of St. Anthony in the Desert, a favourite theme in these monasteries. There are other figures on the bottom left-hand side, which may depict a hunting scene. The striking ring-chain motif on the back of the shaft is known to be a particularly popular pattern used on the Isle of Man during the 10th century.

From the end of the 10th century onwards Norse raids on religious houses gradually declined as the Norsemen converted to Christianity. Some even came to Anglesey for religious instruction and to take holy orders, a fact which may account for Ynys Seiriol becoming known as Priestholm.

In 1995 the first evidence of a Viking settlement was found on Anglesey. The site, close to Red Wharf Bay, a natural harbour, would have been an ideal landing stage between the Viking centres at Dublin and York. There is no evidence to link this settlement with Ingimund, but late 8th and 9th century coins have been discovered, and radiocarbon dated charcoal from the settlement, to the same period. The settlement consists of two large Viking type halls, and another building, as well as evidence of farming, iron forging and bronze and antler crafts. There is also evidence of trading as six weights and quantities of hacksilver (fragments of silver cut up to be used in exchange for goods) have been found. However the most unusual and fascinating find is a large whetstone, with a bronze ferrule and one end in the shape of a pointed Viking helmet, attached to a ring. According to an archaeologist from the National Museum of Wales, the whetstone has been little used and appears to have been more a symbol of rank than a working object. A tenth century alloy pin and a small bronze bell, possibly worn as part of a women's dress, were also found.

An interesting theory is proposed by the historian, Mr B.G Charles in his Old Norse Relations with Wales, concerning the great number of raids on Wales.

'There is reason to believe,' Old Norse Relations with Wales, 'that the object of a great number of raids on Wales was the capture of prisoners of war for transportation on the slave markets of the various trading centres which the Scandinavians regularly visited.'

Whether there is any truth in this theory of slave trade has not been proven, but we do know that in 987 Godfrey Haroldson took two thousand prisoners from Môn when he intervened on behalf of Cadwallon ap Ieuaf. Two years later the Welsh Chronicle recorded that Maredudd ap Owain, grandson of Hywel Dda, was compelled to exchange those men he had taken captive for one penny a head. There are many other instances in records that support the slave-trade claim, but no firm evidence.

There was still no respite from the violent Viking raids, and the year 999 saw the death of Maredudd ab Owain who had succeeded in reuniting Deheubarth and Gwynedd during his reign.

Throughout the 10th-11th centuries the conflicting battles between Môn and Ireland continued, and when one branch of Rhodri Mawr's line, Gruffudd ap Llywelyn, took control of Gwynedd from Cynan in 1039, Cynan fled to Dublin, which was then a Viking city. Gruffudd ap Llywelyn did what his great ancestors Hywel Dda and Rhodri Mawr could not do. He succeeded in uniting the whole of Wales; Gwynedd, Powys, Deheubarth, Morgannwg and Gwent into one kingdom. One of Gruffudd's first achievements was to attack the men of Mercia between Welshpool and Shrewsbury. The assault was unexpected, and the Mercians were destroyed, and their leader Edwin, brother of Leofric and brother-in-law of Lady Godiva, was killed. Thirteen years later, Gruffydd gained a further victory at Leominister proving that he could beat the English even on their own soil. This affected the Normans greatly because they had soldiers in the English army, and now under the direction of Edward the Confessor, the Normans were gaining more control of England. Gruffudd was aware of them as a potential danger to the people of Wales and this was one of the reasons for the attack. But this initial success was not to last. In 1063 Earl Harold of Wessex took advantage of a temporary weakness in Mercia and quickly marched through the kingdom to attack the Welsh leader's stronghold at Rhuddlan. North Wales was ravaged whilst Gruffudd escaped by sea, and sadly died at the hands of one of his own followers. His head was sent as a trophy to the man who had organized his killing, Harold Goodwinson, later Harold II.

CHAPTER THIRTEEN

THE AGE OF THE CASTLE

The year 1066 is familiar to us all, and although William the Conqueror did not cross the sea to conquer Wales, the Norman invasion soon had its effect on the Welsh kingdoms. In order to protect his own realms, William encouraged his knights to take on lordships for themselves, especially along the borders (the marches) of Wales. The Welsh, now weakened by internal dynastic quarrels, were a sitting target for the new Marcher Warlords who swept across the border counties, but the Norman attack on North Wales did not fair so well. There they encountered a new leader, the half Welsh and half Irish\Viking, called Gruffudd ap Cynan who had arrived from Ireland to re-establish the powerful kingdom of Gwynedd, which was to cause problems for the Normans for the next two hundred years.

His first attempt to gain the kingdom, in 1075, failed because to the Welsh he was just another Viking raider, and he could not count on their support. Two years later he tried again and after landing at Abermenai, quickly took possession of Môn and Arfon. Soon disputes broke out amongst the invaders because Gruffudd ap Cynan would not allow them to loot the country-side. A skirmish broke out and he forced the unruly army back to Ireland after they ran amok in Môn.

In 1081 a third attempt was made. This time he set sail with a fleet of ships which had been presented to him and equipped by King Dermont of Dublin. He landed at Porth Clais, a mile from Ty Ddewi (St David's) in the south, and joined forces with Rhys ap Tewdwr. A decisive battle was fought on Mynydd Carn, the site of which has still not been identified, although evidence suggests that it was around the middle or eastern end of the Preseli mountain range. Triumphantly they pushed towards North Wales and captured Gwynedd, but this success was not to last. Within a short time, the Norman Earls, Hugh of Chester and Roger of Montgomery had taken Gruffudd captive, and imprisoned him and many of his supporters in Chester jail.

By 1086 the Earl of Chester, and his cousin, Robert of Rhuddlan, were well established east of Afon Clwyd, and had founded castles at Deganwy, Bangor, Caernarfon and at Aberlleiniog on the Isle of Anglesey.

Aberlleiniog castle would have been built of wood in the motte style. Today in a wood not far from the coast at Penmon, the remains of this castle may be reached along an unmarked path. The site is difficult to find because all that is visible is a mound, topped by the low but sturdy remains of a stone castle which replaced the original.

After this initial success, Norman control in North Wales was short lived. We know that Gruffudd ap Cynan made an escape attempt in 1087, and the following year raided the Norman territories and killed Robert of Rhuddlan. Later he attacked and defeated the Normans in Môn with a fleet of ships that had been equipped by Godfrey Mearanach. By 1094 Gruffudd ap Cynan had regained his freedom and with the help of his mother's relations, drove the Norman earls out. All the castles west of Deganwy were stormed and Aberlleiniog castle was captured. The custodian of the castle, together with about 120 knights were taken prisoner. This was a major set back for the Norman army and it made them abandon their plan to capture Môn.

In 1098 the Earls of Chester and Shrewsbury marched through North Wales to Môn. Gruffudd ap Cynan enlisted the support of a fleet of Viking vessels from Ireland, but the Vikings proved to be disloyal. One vessel and its crew joined the Norman cause when they were offered better terms and ravaged and pillaged Môn whilst its leaders fled to Ireland. But help was at hand and a fleet, under Magnus Barefoot King of Norway, appeared on the scene, won the battle of Môn and killed the Earl of Shrewsbury, forcing the Norman soldiers to retreat to Chester. Magnus and his fleet disappeared as quickly as they came, although he did return in 1102 to plunder Mon's timber to build castles on the Isle of Man, but little came of this skirmish. Obviously the Norman's did not realize the potential or the importance of the island as they did not try to attack Môn again. In 1099 the exiled prince was able to return, and Gruffudd ap Cynan took possession, abandoning his role as a Viking chief in order to claim his rightful inheritance.

The years between 1094-1137 – the reign of Gruffudd ap Cynan were the most peaceful for Welsh independence, and a time when the princes absorbed many of the fashionable European reforming ideas and adapted effective plans for both state and church affairs.

When Gruffudd ap Cynan died in 1137, at the grand age of 82, his son Owain Gwynedd inherited a secure and prosperous Môn. During this time England was engaged in civil war, and Owain used his skills as a statesman and soldier to extend his frontiers. This has often been referred to as the Golden Age of Welsh Independence. Everyone recognized Owain Gwynedd's success and he became known as Owain Fawr.

It was a time of much excitement too as more monastic foundations were being encouraged and the diocesan boundaries were being more finely defined, so that many new stone churches were being built. Motte and bailey earthwork castles, identical to those built by the Norman invaders, were being copied and erected by the princes at the centre of their own estates, and such fine works as the arch at Aberffraw and the original priory church at Penmon were built. Two of Owain's sons were credited with building the first stone castle in Gwynedd.

In 1154, Henry II had succeeded to the English throne, and for a while, left Wales alone. However, after spending a year in France, he returned to England in April 1157 and turned his attentions to Wales and led his first campaign aganst Owain. The task of depriving Owain Gwynedd of his land seemed an easy one for Henry. He set out from Chester with a strong army, but in an encounter with the Welsh Henry narrowly escaped death in battle at Tal Moelfre, Anglesey. His illegitimate son was killed and his half brother was badly injured. The battle ended in a truce and Owain was wise enough to pay homage to the king. For a number of years Owain continued to rule in peace and adopted the title of Tywysog Cymru (Prince of The Welsh).

But sadly as we have seen so many times throughout Welsh history, when Owain died in 1170 he was not followed immediately by a strong ruler. Upon his death war broke out between his sons. Dafydd and Rhodri killed their half brother Hywel, and for the next twenty years Gwynedd was divided between them. However south Wales became dominant under Rhys ap Gruffudd Yr Arglwydd (Lord) Rhys; and by 1194 Gwynedd once again had a powerful and effective prince when Llywelyn ap Iorwerth (Fawr) defeated his uncle Dafydd ap Owain Gwynedd and gained control. Llywelyn was the grandson of Owain Gwynedd and became the most important Welsh ruler of the first half of the thirteenth century. During his reign, he constructed stone castles, sited at points on the periphery of Snowdonia to protect the great Môn store-cupboard. But when he died in 1240, Gwynedd was again threatened by a disputed inheritance and a renewed interest from England. It was only when his grandson, Llywelyn ap Gruffudd (Llywelyn II), overcame the family rivalry in 1255 that the political legacy of Llywelyn Fawr began to be rebuilt by a combination of raids and alliances. Llywelyn II's position as ruler of Wales – as far south as Caerphilly – was eventually recognized on 25 September 1267 by Henry III, in the treaty of Montgomery. This was the first time that an English King had acknowledged the title Prince of Wales, and the idea of Wales as a unified state.

In 1274 Henry III was succeeded by his more effective son, Edward I. Llywelyn's brothers and their allies soon began to make trouble for Llywelyn II and the new English King. He also added to his own difficulties by refusing to attend the coronation, and by ignoring a series of summonses to pay homage to the king. Finally war was declared in 1276, and the first campaigns centred around the Severn and Dee valleys. Llywelyn was forced to retreat and Edward I constructed new castles at Flint and Rhuddlan. When the Peace treaty of Aberconway was agreed in 1277, Llywelyn lost almost all he had gained some ten years earlier. This was partly because Edward 1 recognized the importance of Môn to the survival of Wales. The island was able to supply the whole country with grain, without which the county could not survive. Edward decided to blockade the corn supply, and to seize the harvest for his own use, by sending in a fleet of ships.

For a while there was a lull in fighting but this did not last long. Llywelyn's brother Dafydd infuriated Edward by launching an attack on Hawarden Castle in March 1282 and also at Oswestry. War began and Llywelyn was pursued and killed at Cilmeri (near Builth Wells) on 11 December of that year. His head was sent as a trophy to the king and his body taken to the abbey at Cwm Hir. Dafydd continued to fight on alone, but now full of confidence, Edward swept down Dyffryn Conwy (valley). In the early summer he captured Dafydd who was hung, drawn and quartered – a new punishment devised by the King for the crime of treason.

This effectively marked the end of the Welsh resistance, but Edward intended to strengthen his victory further. During the months of July and August 1283 he visited Anglesey and stayed at Rhosyr, Aberffraw, Caergybi, Penrhosllugwy and Llan-faes. In March 1284 the Statute of Rhuddlan was instituted which abolished much of Welsh native law and Môn became one of the three new counties in North Wales, with its own sheriff and county court.

When Edward I's son, another Prince Edward, later Edward II, was born at Caernarfon he was presented to the Welsh people as their new Prince of Wales and the practise of granting this title to the English Monarch's eldest son continues to this day.

On 11 April 1295 Edward crossed from Bangor to Llan-faes, which he had made his headquarters. He stayed three weeks and it was during this stay that he embarked on one of the most ambitious and expensive castle and borough building programmes that Europe had ever witnessed. Over the next twelve years he spent sixty thousand pounds (about one and a half million pounds in to-day's terms and more than ten times his annual income), on building castles and walled towns at Conwy, Caernarfon, Harlech and Beaumaris.

The programme was financed by Tuscan bankers and executed by a chief architect from Savoy. The castles, each designed precisely to the site where they were to be built, were the work of one man, Master James of St George. He was born about 1230, and had worked on a number of great European castles including the fortress of St George d'Esperanche (in Savoy on the French/Swiss/Italian border) from which he took his name. Master James was directly responsible for at least twelve of the seventeen castles in Wales which Edward either built, rebuilt or strengthened.

Beaumaris was his last and by now he had perfected the concentric design. The single strong keep was no longer considered to be sufficient. Instead it was thought that defence lay in tactically designed walls – often two circuits with walls within walls – giving advantageous coverage of the line of fire, and which was to characterize the castles of the time.

Edward I decided that Beaumaris was to be his headquarters and was determined that he would have a completely English town. He moved the inhabitants to the other end of the strait, to a new town which he called Newborough and to which he gave a Royal charter. We can all imagine the heart-break and unhappiness this must have caused by uprooting the community, but when we consider that he could just as easily have turned everyone out without making any arrangements for their well-being, his actions don't seem so heartless.

Beaumaris was built on a low flat site near Llan-faes, whose important role as a commercial centre and port was to be transferred to the English borough of Beaumaris. In sole charge of the operation was Master James, who was by now in his late fifties, and already a builder of seven Welsh castles. Two hundred quarrymen, four hundred masons, thirty smiths and carpenters and an army of two thousand labourers were employed on the project. In addition, thirty boats, sixty wagons, and one hundred carts were used to bring stone to the site, and to transport coal for the lime kilns.

The site was undeveloped and had no rocky foundation to dictate the plan. Consequently it is the most perfectly symmetrical of Master James' concentric designs, and is considered to be the most sophisticated example of medieval military architecture in Britain. Never before had so much royal money been spent on one single operation. In the first six months of construction, huge sums of money totalling six thousand pounds were invested on this castle. Yet despite this, Beaumaris Castle was never finished, and the ground plan for a spectacular fortress was never realized.

The town grew up around the castle. It's name, Beaumaris, is derived from the Norman-French Beau Marais, meaning beautiful marsh, but it has also been suggested that the name originated from Bi Maras, the place where two tides or two seas meet. It was once known as Porth Wygyr, partly of Viking origin. Beaumaris is also mentioned in the Welsh triads as one of the three main seaports in the British kingdoms after the Saxon conquest.

King Edward appointed a Gascon knight, Sir William Pickmore, to be the first constable of the castle. He was also made Captain of the Town, an office which it became customary for the Constable to hold. The constables annual fee was £40, and the Captains £12.3s.4d. The garrison received four pence per week on market day in Rations Row, hence the origin of the road now known as Rating Row.

Today portable audio tapes offer an excellent guide to the building, and are a must to gain full benefit from your visit. There is also an exhibition on the architecture and history of the castle on display in the Chapel Tower. Summer entertainment includes jousting and medieval fairs.

CHAPTER FOURTEEN

MEDIEVAL ANGLESEY

After Edward I's conquest, Gwynedd, west of Conwy was divided into three shires – Môn, Caernarfon and Merioneth. All three shires remained in the hands of the Crown and were, in fact, simply royal lordships in disguise.

The commote (cwmwd), a subdivision of a cantref which was the basic unit of local administration under the princes of Gwynedd, was retained. This usually corresponded in size to an English Hundred, and came under the authority of the chief royal official, the sheriff. He had two key roles – one judicial and the other as financial officer. In his judicial role he presided over the county court which, according to records, met once a month (on a Thursday) at Beaumaris. Like all courts of law it dealt with the punishment of crime and the upkeep of law and order. The sheriff selected a jury, consisting of five members of the community.

In his financial role he was responsible for the collection of all royal revenue, such as the rents from the various commotes. He was also accountable for the profits of justice such as fines levied by the different courts. Some income came from escheat lands, property that came into the possession of the Crown following the death of the landowner in the absence of any legal heirs. There was also a small amount of revenue from wrecks around the coast of the island, and from goods and chattels acquired from vagrants, convicted criminals and those who died intestate. The sheriff was also responsible for any arrears from the previous years, and was expected to meet those not collected out of his own pocket!

The second official was the coroner, and although this office had existed in England from the 12th century, very little is known of its existence in Wales before this period. According to the Statute of Rhuddlan there were two coroners for each county. In Môn, one was responsible for Talbolian, Twrcelyn and Dindaethwy and the other for Llifon, Malltraeth and Menai. The duties consisted of viewing all the bodies of those who had died from misadventure, or were so badly injured that there was no hope of recovery. After viewing the body, the coroner would hold an inquest with a jury selected from the community where the death had occurred, as well as people from the four adjoining communities.

This period, from the conquest of Edward I to the accession of Henry Tudor in 1485 is more obscure than of any other period in Welsh history. Even today many aspects of Medieval Anglesey remain a mystery to us, although it is possible from records to pick out snippets of information which help us to create a picture in our minds of the economy and life within Medieval Angelsey.

We do know that the people of Wales were not happy under the rule of Edward I but in time relapsed into a despondent acceptance of the situation. Soon this lack of hope and courage was to be reflected by the Welsh poets or bards, who, following the conquest, had lost some of their status. Once they wrote about war and the great heroes of Wales, now the next generation began to write melancholy poems about the beauty of Wales, the solitude, and the woodlands.

The Welsh saw very little of the future Edward II, their first English 'Prince of Wales', until he succeeded to the throne in 1301. Prior to this he was fully occupied in his father's Scottish campaign, and the administration of Môn had been left unsuccessfully to the officials. On his accession to the throne he was able to build up a strong group of officials who were loyal to him and were upset when he was captured whilst fleeing from his wife, Isabel, and subsequently murdered.

The Welsh had always been a fiery nation and some Welshmen still hankered after war. Some seven thousand men from Wales were raised for the Crècy campaign of 1346, and it was thanks to five thousand Welsh longbow-men, that the Battle of Crècy was won. They were dressed in green and white and this is thought to have been the first time that troops wore a uniform on a continental battlefield.

Those that stayed at home worked in the fields and with animals. Wheat and barley was harvested in Môn, but oats was the dominant crop. Sheep were kept for wool, meat, and milk which was often made into cheese, whilst oxen were kept for meat and leather. It has been estimated that the average household in Môn had two oxen, eleven sheep, six bushels of wheat, twenty-six bushels of oats and three bushels of barley.

With so much grain being produced it is hardly surprising to learn that one of the most important products to any agricultural community, the millstone, was quarried in Môn, principally from Mathafarn Eithaf, Mathafarn Wion and Penmon. Carboniferous limestone was the best millstone and many were exported to the mills at Dublin, Meirionnydd, and Chester.

As well as Môn millstone, the main exports were wool, dairy products and timber. The most valuable import was wine and leading ports , like Beaumaris, had their own ships and an extensive foreign trade. Thanks to this trade Môn is considered by some to have been richer during this period than many parts of England.

The most important manufacturing industry in the medieval period was the weaving of cloth, and records reveal a number of weavers operating in Anglesey. Much of the local cloth would have been sold at fairs held at Beaumaris, Llannerch-y-medd, Aberffraw and Newborough (Niwbwrch). In the accounts of 1350-1351 there appears an amount of 10s 6d for tolls collected on Welsh cloths at the two Llannerch-y-medd fairs.

Fish also formed a vital part of the medieval diet and towards the end of the 13th century a flourishing herring fishery was centred on Llan-faes. There are also references to fisheries and the port at Beaumaris.

By the end of the 13th century the increase in population had reduced the amount of land available for farming. The climate too had worsened, and with much colder and wetter weather, poorer harvests with a high risk of famine were inevitable. Between 1315 and 1317 the harvest failed for three consecutive years, thus affecting the food supply as well as the seed-corn for the following year. This was followed by a series of livestock epidemics as well as a steady decline in farming prices.

The increase in rainfall also caused its problems by changing the sea level with devastating results. It has been recorded that on 6 December 1330 part of the commote of Menai was struck by a violent storm. One hundred and eighty-three acres of land in the borough of Newborough was engulfed by the sea and sand, and at Rhosyr eleven cottages and twenty-eight acres of land suffered the same fate. This particular area of the island has always been at risk from sand and today is managed by the Forestry Commission who hold the dunes in check.

Interestingly, in the summer of 1996, one of the royal courts of the 13th century Princes of Gwynedd was uncovered, buried deep in the sand, at Rhosyr. The court is the best preserved of the royal courts and at least three major buildings have been found, as well as various other constructions and a long stretch of a perimeter wall. One of the buildings was once a large hall with an off-centre hearth, with a range of adjoining rooms leading off from the main hall.

There is no doubt about its royal connections because, as we have seen, Gwynedd was divided into a number of administration areas, each containing a royal township, and from the documented records we know that one existed at Rhosyr.

However, what is interesting is the fact that the excavations suggest that the Princes of Gwynedd did not enjoy a luxurious lifestyle. The buildings are simple and the main hall appears to have been built of timber, and one of the other buildings has rounded corners, which suggests that it had a thatched roof.

The finds were small and included ring brooches, a spur, strap-ends, a small knife and coins, which does not indicate great wealth. Perhaps further excavations will reveal more of interest in the future.

Another catastrophe to hit Medieval Môn was the Black Plague (Y Farwolaeth Fawr), or bubonic plague. This deadly disease began in central Asia and was carried along the trade routes into Europe, reaching Britain in 1348. It first appeared in Wales in the spring of 1349 where as many as one hundred thousand people died from the disease during the coming years. Môn did not escape.

Môn and Caernarfonshire were so badly affected that the Môn poet Gruffudd ap Maredudd ap Dafydd begged God to show mercy to Gwynedd. No one is sure how the plague spread to Môn, but an income report for Beaumaris port, dated 1350-1351, recorded eight-pence being received from two foreign ships. Perhaps the cause of the Black Plague?

The most probable cause of the plague was the migration of people. There had always been a movement of people during harvest time, but now immigrants could be placed under the protection of the prince or apply for an order for permanent settlement. This became common-place in Europe following the plague and it gave many a chance to better themselves. Labour was scarce and the fittest and strongest were able to demand higher wages, which employers were willing to pay.

The effects of the Plague took its toll on the communities. There was an immediate drop in revenue because of the high death rate among bondmen who paid heavier rents. Before the plague the authorities had no difficulty in finding tenants for escheat lands, but now they had a glut of untenanted land, which resulted in much of the arable land being let for grazing. Enterprising individuals were able to acquire vacant land cheaply and this contributed to the growth of new estates, as well as a new breed of landed gentry.

The economic strength of an area can usually be determined by the health of its inhabitants, but little is known about sickness during this period, especially concerning its prevention and cure. Records give us no clues, except about those who were shunned by society – the lepers. Leprosy had a long history in Wales, and in Welsh law it was recognised as one of the grounds for a divorce. There were many leper institutions set up around the country, but none in Anglesey, although it appears that there were houses set aside for lepers. One house was recorded in every commote except Penrhosllugwy. In 1381 the account books show a sum of two shillings, the profits of a house and three acres of land at Aberffraw, which were now in the king's possession because there were no lepers there. However, we do learn that one leper, Gruffudd ap Hywel Ddu occupied it in the year 1386-1387. The fact that some of the houses were empty could indicate that the condition was not common in Anglesey, but we have no firm records to prove this theory.

The fourteenth century was also a time of political tension in Wales. During the second half of the century the last heir to the Gwynedd dynasty, Owain ap Thomas ap Rhodri, made a bid to claim his inheritance. He was the great-nephew of Llywelyn ap Gruffudd, and was also know as Owain Lawgoch (Red Hand). His grandfather, Llywelyn's youngest brother had sold his rights to Gwynedd and had retired to England as a royal pensioner. It appears that Owain himself had spent his youth abroad, and had returned in 1363 after his father's death to claim his inheritance, but in 1369 the lands were confiscated because he formed an allegiance with the French where he commanded a company of Welshmen. To the French he was known as Yvain de Galles. After the renewal of hostilities in 1369, Charles V and his advisors saw the possibility of an invasion of Wales and a revolt, and were willing to back an attack on Owain's behalf.

At the end of 1369 an expedition set out under Owain's command from Harfleur, but was driven back by storms. Another attempt was made in 1372, but they were attacked at Guernsey. For the next few years he continued to campaign against the English in south-west France, and in the summer of 1378 besieged the fortress of Mortagne-sur-Gironde where an English agent, John Lambe, assassinated him. He had tricked his way into Owain's service and was paid £20 for killing him. This ended the direct line of the Gwynedd dynasty, although many found his death hard to accept, and he became known as the 'Sleeping Hero'. This resulted in many folk-tales which have survived to the present time and tell of Owain Lawgoch, asleep in a cave, waiting for a call to claim his inheritance.

This was also the period of another Owain, the famous rebel, Owain ap Gruffudd Fychan or Owain Glyndŵr, Lord of Glyndyfrdwy and Cynllaith Owain. He was a landowner of noble Welsh ancestry, who was educated in London and proclaimed Prince of Wales at Glyndyfrdwy in Merionnydd, on 16 September 1400. He embarked on a rebellion that lasted for fifteen years and caused devastation throughout Wales. This was the last attempt to regain Welsh independence and, although ultimately unsuccessful, Owain Glyndŵr became one of the national heroes of Wales.

Tradition relates that the cause of the revolt was a boundary dispute between Owain and his neighbour Reginald de Grey, lord of Dyffryn Clwyd. However, it is more likely that they had been planning a revolt for some time, and a key role may have been played by the sons of Tudur Goronwy of Penmynydd who were descendants of Ednyfed Fychan. Like all revolts there were winners and losers, but no one person seems to have emerged as a great victor of the revolt.

Many historians believe that the end of the Glyndŵr revolt in 1415 marked both an end and a beginning for Wales. National awareness was strengthened for the first time and more of Wales was united than ever before. Yet despite all the tragedies, with the economic chaos that followed the Black Death, and the aftermath of the revolt of Owain Glyndŵr, the fifteenth century saw the expansion of towns and landed estates. Sadly, few of these medieval houses have survived in Môn although at least one may be found in Beaumaris. Also, at Llansadwrn, Hafoty, once the home of the Norris family, may date from the late 14th or early 15th century, whilst the hall at Plas Boderwyd is probably of a late medieval period. Although there was plenty of building stone in Môn, most of the houses were probably built of mud and clay and thatched with straw. Timber was not easily available on the island, and had to be brought from the mainland.

This was the period that saw many family estates begin to grow, and one of the richest families in north Wales at the time was the Griffith family of Penrhyn, near Bangor. Gwilym ap Gruffudd had, by 1405, made his peace with the authorities and founded a family which was to dominate the north until the middle of the 16th century. Through his first marriage he acquired the seat of Ednyfed Fychan of Penmynydd, and his second marriage to one of the Stanleys, a leading Cheshire family, gave him more land. By the time he died in 1431 he was probably the richest man in north Wales. However, not all his wealth was gained through marriage as he appears to have been involved in extensive business dealings. According to a list of his debtors in 1406, he was dealing in money lending, hiring out cattle and oxen, as well as trading in wine and buying up tithes. After his death Gwilym's son, Gwilym Fychan (or William Griffith), carried on building up the estate, and created a new estate at Plas Newydd, for one of his illegitimate sons.

Another famous North Wales family were the Bulkeleys who came from Cheadle in Cheshire. William Bulkeley the elder, born in 1418, settled in Beaumaris and created one of the largest estates in Angelsey. We are not sure why he came to settle in Anglesey but it appears that he was already a wealthy man and heir to an estate in Cheadle worth about forty pound per annum. However, it was through his marriage to Elen, daughter of Gwilym ap Gruffudd that he really became established. Between them they set about acquiring other lands in Anglesey, and when their son married the daughter and heiress of Bartholomew de Bolde, a Conwy burgess, the Bulkeley family came to own land there too. William was a prominent figure in the community and in 1448 was appointed the king's sergeant-in-arms for Angelsey. Between 1452 and 1453 he was deputy-constable of Beaumaris Castle and from 1473 to 1489 he was Alderman of the borough, and also a member of various commissions.

The centre of the Bulkeley's power was the town of Beaumaris, and in the last quarter of the century he built Henblas, probably the largest house in Beaumaris, near the church. This became their principal seat until they moved to Baron Hill in the beginning of the 17th century. Henblas was eventually demolished during the 19th century.

When William died in 1490 he left twenty pounds in his will for a tomb for himself and his wife, as well as money for books and vestments for Beaumaris Church. The tomb inside the church contains a fine pair of alabaster figures supposedly of William and his wife, but some historians believe this to be the tomb of Roland Bulkeley, their son, who died in 1537, and his wife Alice. However, on close inspection, the visitor will notice that the dress on the figure is definitely late 15th century.

The parish church of St Mary and St Nicholas in the centre of the town is full of reminders of the Bulkeley family. The most interesting relics are the coverstone and coffin of Siwan (Princess Joan), wife of Llywelyn ap Iorwerth (Llywelyn Fawr), and the illegitimate daughter of King John of England. This is situated in the south porch and is one of the finest stone carvings in north Wales. The effigy shows the head and shoulders of the princess, wearing a wimple – a piece of cloth draped around the head to frame the face, worn by women in the Middle Ages, and which is still part of the habit of some nuns today. The head is capped with a coronet, and the hands are raised in prayer. The rest of the slab is covered in floral decoration, which includes a stem of a flower held in the mouth of a wyvern, a mythical bird, whose tail is knotted and entwined in the foliage, and which is worth a closer look.

As you can imagine, the town of Beaumaris was dominated by its castle, which was frequently used as a prison. Records show that between 1318 and 1328 the castle held three prisoners; Patrick mac Coter, Stephan mac Steffan and Andrew mac Orlot, who were sometimes described as Manxmen and sometimes as Scotsmen. They were each allowed three-pence a day and may have been released as a result of the Anglo-Scottish Treaty of Northampton, which was signed in 1329. In 1395 a number of Lollard prisoners included three who were fellows of Merton College, Oxford, and one of whom was an ecclesiastical lawyer, were sent to Beaumaris.

In 1449 the most famous prisoner arrived from the Isle of Man. She was Eleanor Cobham, widow of Henry's VI's uncle, Humphrey, Duke of Gloucester, who had been condemned to life imprisonment for witchcraft in 1441. Three years later on 7 July 1452 she died, and it is presumed that she is buried at the parish church.

CHAPTER FIFTEEN

THE TUDOR DYNASTY

It is from Goronwy ap Ednyfed that the Tudurs of Penmynydd were descended. Some historians believe that the name Tudur first appeared in Môn when Ednyfed Fychan, Llywelyn Fawr's right hand man, used it as a Christian name for one of his sons. Others believe that Owain, the grandson of Goronwy was the first in the family to adopt the surname Tudur.

The old stone manor house of Plas Penmynydd stands a little way outside the village of Penmynydd, just off the A5420. Sadly, although this house is on the same spot and has the same name, it the not actually the house in which Owain was born. The house you see today was built around 1576, presumably on the site of an earlier medieval homestead. It was largely rebuilt in the 17th century, with further additions made in the 19th century. However, if the visitor looks closely they will see that the house still bears the Tudor arms on its exterior. Plas Penmynydd, or at least the original old farmstead, was where Owain ap Maredudd ap Tudur ap Goronwy Fychan, otherwise known as Owain Tudur, and grandfather of Henry VII, was born in 1385. He was brought up by his uncle Gronw, because his father, Maredudd, was a political fugitive. He was an exceptionally handsome young man, who eventually joined the household of Henry IV and distinguishing himself in the royal Court of Windsor. It is possible that he was introduced to the household by his great friend Maredudd, son of Owain Glyndŵr who was already a courtier there. In the English court he was known as Owen Tudor, although in Anglesey he became known as 'The Rose of Mona' because of his good looks and his nobility.

It was not long before Owain attracted the attention of the young Queen mother, Katherine de Valois, daughter of the French king Charles VI, and widow of Henry V. Obviously there were suspicions concerning their relationship as a parliamentary decree, passed in 1427, had enacted that a marriage with a queen-dowager without the consent of parliament would be considered illegal. Despite this act, Owain was determined to marry, and he and Katherine were secretly married, probably around 1429, a fact that was a well kept secret until Katherine's death.

It seems that Owain took his wife to Anglesey to proudly introduce her to his friends and relatives but, although they welcomed the couple, the meeting did not go well. The inhabitants of Anglesey spoke no French or English and must have remained silent throughout the visit, for it is claimed that Katherine later remarked that they were 'the goodliest dumb creatures that she ever knew'.

The couple lived happily and quietly out of the public eye, and had three sons, Edmund, Jasper and Thomas, but Thomas died young after a short time as a monk at Westminster. A daughter Jacina, possibly became the wife of Lord Grey de Wilton, and another daughter, Margaret, died a few days after her birth in 1436.

Katherine either went to, or was sent to, the Abbey at Bermondsey where she died. Her epitaph made no mention of the fact that she was the wife of Owain. After her death Owain was summoned before the Privy Council and charged with marrying a queen-dowager without the consent of parliament. He refused to appear and took sanctuary at Westminster. He was then accused of being disloyal and left the sanctuary to protest his innocence. He was immediately arrested, imprisoned in Newgate Prison, escaped and was recaptured. He escaped a second time and made his way to Wales where he took up arms against the king. Later a reconciliation took place and finally, in 1439, his stepson Henry VI, granted him a full pardon.

Although no official title was ever granted to Owain he was made 'keeper of our parks in Denbigh'. Much later he led a royalist army against the Yorkists and was defeated at Mortimer's cross in 1461. He was taken a prisoner and beheaded in Hereford's Market Place.

After Katherine's death Owain was deprived custody of the children and we know that Edmund and Jasper were placed in the care of the Abbess of Barking. In 1440 Henry VI began to show a personal interest in the education and welfare of his step-brothers, which they repaid by becoming loyal supporters of the King. In 1452 Edmund was given the title of Earl of Richmond, and at the same time Jasper was created Earl of Pembroke. Edmund married a young thirteen-year-old heiress, Margaret Beaufort, the daughter of the Earl of Somerset and a descendant of the Lancastrian John of Gaunt. When Edmund was fighting in the Wars of the Roses, Margaret was taken to Pembroke castle by Jasper for protection. Later Edmund was imprisoned at Caerfyrddin (Carmarthen) and, although released after a couple of days, died a few weeks later of tuberculosis, most probably picked up whilst in custody. Two months later, on the 28th January, 1457, his posthumous son, Henry, Earl of Richmond was born. Through his mother being a descendant of John of Gaunt, he was able later to claim the throne of England to become Henry VII.

Edmund's death prevented him from playing a major role in the Wars of the Roses, but Jasper became a firm friend of Henry VI, and in the years that followed, Jasper's opinions were greatly valued by the Lancastrians.

The events that led up to the defeat of Richard III on Bosworth field in 1485 are well known, and it is sufficient to say that it was on the battle field, and with Richard's crown, that Henry was crowned King Henry VII. This fulfilled an ancient prophecy.by Myrddin (Merlin) the wizard, that one day a prince of Welsh blood from Môn would succeed to the throne of England.

Henry VII had the epitaph on his grandmother Katherine's tomb replaced by one that acknowledged her marriage to his grandfather Owain. But perhaps the most odd epilogue to the story of Katherine concerns her body, which was later exhumed. It was claimed that it could be seen and touched 'by anyone who much desire it.' Tradition claims that this was her own wish and her voluntary penance for her 'disobedience' to her husband, for being delivered of her son, Henry VI, at Windsor, a place he forbade. Interestingly Samuel Pepys's entry in his diary for February 23rd 1669 records:

' . . . to Westminster Abbey, and there did see all the tombs very finely... and there we did see, by particular favour, the body of Queen Katherine de Valois; and I had the upper part of her body in my hands, and I did kiss her mouth, reflecting upon it that I did kiss a Queen, and that this was my birth-day. Thirty-six years old, that I did kiss a Queen.'

Her body was finally laid to rest in 1716.

Henry VII (Harri Tudur) had been born in Wales, nursed by a Welsh foster-mother and spoke Welsh fluently. He had a passion for Wales, its history and genealogy and employed one of the best genealogists in the country to establish the ancestry of his grandfather Owain Tudur. He named his eldest son Arthur, after the legendary King Arthur, and every Welshman was looking forward to the day when 'Arthur the once and future king' would return. Henry hoped this would gain him the respect of the Welsh people, but things did not work out as planned. Arthur married Catherine of Spain but he was not a strong man and, within a year of his marriage, he died. Henry was broken-hearted but determined to keep the Tudor dynasty going. After a special edict from the Pope, the newly widowed Catherine of Aragon was married to Arthur's younger brother Henry, and she became the first of the six wives of the future Henry VIII.

Henry VII was a flamboyant King who wore fabulous clothes and jewels. He was the first monarch to be described by the word majesty, which then entered the English language. He also started the Yeoman of the Guard, and had many Welshmen in his court. Henry VII always observed St David's day and records show that in 1492 he gave the Welshmen in his court the equivalent of two pounds to celebrate their national Day. The day ended with a traditional Noson Lawen – an evening entertainment of poetry, song and dance.

Although his reign was important in Welsh history, Henry VII did little for Wales and never returned after his visit in 1485. However, on his deathbed in 1509 he ordered his son Henry VIII to repay his debt to Wales and care for the welfare of the Welsh subjects. When Henry VIII acceded to the throne he claimed to be too busy to spare a thought for the people of Wales. However, in the middle of the 1530's he authorized his chief minister Thomas Cromwell, to look at the needs of Wales, and to reorganize the whole government in Wales. The two most important acts, passed in 1536 and 1543, united Wales with England while making English the only legal language of the Courts and of Government in Wales. But the last Tudor, Queen Elizabeth I, Henry's daughter, authorized the use of the Welsh Prayer Book and a Welsh Bible, at a time when she was trying to impose a single religious standard throughout the land.

Another building worth a visit, with interesting connections to the Tudurs is Penmynydd Church. It is 14th century, but some of the chevron stones are believed to come from an earlier 12th century building. It is likely that the first building on the site was made of wattle and daub and was erected as early as the 6th century. Its founder is believed to have been Saint Gredifael, a 6th century Celtic saint, to whom the church is dedicated. The Tudur chapel contains a memorial to Gronw Tudur (the guardian of Owain) and his wife Myfanwy. It is said that Gronw was drowned in Kent only a few days after being made Forester of Snowdonia and Constable of Beaumaris Castle. His body was brought back to Anglesey and buried in the Friary at Llan-faes. When the monasteries were dissolved, the tomb was removed to its present site. The finely carved alabaster effigies of Gronw and his wife, lay on the alter tomb which bears some shields showing the Tudur arms. These are present on the surcoat of the knight. Although the public can see the effigies, they cannot be touched because the alabaster has been badly damaged in the past by people who have scraped off portions in the belief that the alabaster was a cure for eye disease. The stained glass window in the chapel combines the red and white roses of the Houses of Lancaster and York, and also includes the court of arms of the Beaufort family. Around the window are the words: 'Undeb fel rhosyn yw ar lan afonydd ac fel tŷ dur ar ben y mynydd': (Unity is like a rose on a river bank and like a house of steel on the top of the mountain.) Penmynydd means mountain top and the words *tŷ dur,* which means house of steel, could be a pun on Tudur.

CHAPTER SIXTEEN

AMLWCH AND COPPER MINING ON PARYS MOUNTAIN

Amlwch, one of the larger market towns of Môn owes its existence to Mynydd Parys.

Mynydd Parys was originally known as Mynydd Trysglwyn, and was probably renamed after Robert Parys, a 15th century Chamberlain of north Wales. He had been given the land as a reward for collecting fines for the crown, and is associated with the Scottish Fraser clan, whose story is told in Hone's Table Book. It is reputed that he was the only brother of Simon, Lord Lovat, who was beheaded for his part in the 1745 rising, and that he fled from Scotland after killing a family enemy who had insulted him at a wedding party. He hid within the Parys mines, and afterwards married a local girl. The couple had one son, who the miners called Lord Lovat, a title inherited by his ancestors until the late nineteenth century.

Mynydd Parys is situated just three kilometres south of Amlwch, where the desolate landscape rises to a height of five hundred feet (one hundred and fifty metres) above sea level. Today the deserted mountain resembles a lunar landscape surrounded by stagnant pools and lakes and full of dangerous shafts. It is barely covered by gorse and moor grass, and looks very insignificant to anyone not familiar with its importance and history. It appears that the mountain was largely composed of copper, hence its more common name, Copper Mountain, with the result that most of the inside of the mountain has been hollowed away. It may surprise visitors to learn that in its day it was the largest copper mining area in Europe and considered to be the Mecca of the copper world. The story of this fascinating mountain is told in Copper Mountain by John Rowlands and is well worth reading.

The privately owned site is accessible but certainly not a safe place for families with young children. Nevertheless, for those who tread carefully and respect its geography, it is worth a visit. A disused windmill which used to assist a steam engine to drain the workings is located on the summit, and can be seen from the road below. The remains of the Cornish engine house and stack of a very early period can also be seen on the eastern side of the mountain.

The mines had been worked intermittently throughout every period of history. It is known that they were worked by the early Britons and Romans, and perhaps were even used during the Middle Ages. We do know that during the 14th century cannons were made largely of iron, but by 1520 they were made out of a type of bronze known as gunmetal, which consisted of 90% copper. Perhaps some of the copper for these guns came from Anglesey?

The observant visitor who wishes to seek, will find hammer stones from the prehistoric age littered around the site, as well as crunching stones of the Roman period, and also more modern relics.

However, the copper extraction that led to its heyday didn't begin until 1579 when we are told that a Mr Medley had opened a 'greate myneral worke in Anglesey' from which he obtained a 'myneral water that made alome and copperas, and transmuted iron into copper.' In 1698 there is mention of the 'Prince's Mine' but its vast riches were still unknown. In fact it was considered hardly worth the expense to extract the small amount of ore estimated to exist.

We can only surmise then, that it was with a certain amount of unwillingness that, in 1764, a partnership formed by Charles Roe, a manufacturer of Macclesfield, agreed to lease the workings together with a mine at Penrhyn Du on the Llyn Peninsula.

After several failed attempts to find ore in profitable quantities, it was decided, in 1768, to make one last attempt to extract ore in paying quantities and the foreman, Rhoose, was sent for. On examining the area he was attracted to a capreous spring and decided to sink a shaft. To encourage his men to work he promised a prize of a bottle of brandy to the first man to strike ore. Work started in earnest and on March 2nd, a rich vein was struck. The lucky prizewinner was Roland Pugh who, not only won his bottle of brandy, but was granted a cottage rent-free for life – a huge reward in any days. He also enjoyed the honour of being 'chaired' at the annual celebration of his discovery.

By now there was a rise in demand for copper, sparked off by naval warfare. It had become the fashion to coat the ships' hulls with a plating of copper just below the waterline. Later, the bolts which secured these plates in place were made of copper too. It is interesting to note that the effectiveness of copper to prevent marine growth on ships hulls was first realised at Amlwch. Vessels trading in and out of Amlwch Harbour were found to remain comparatively free from troubles. A study was carried out and it was discovered that the ships using the harbour had become immune to the effects of marine life. Further investigation revealed that this had occurred because of the strong solution of copper salts in the streams which had their source high up in the region of Mynydd Parys.

In 1775 ore was struck further west and a second mine was opened. The number of shafts were small as most of the ore was being quarried in the open, with as much as eight tons of gunpowder being used in a year to blast the ore from the rocks. Although still a small industry, it has been said that many thousand of tons of copper ore could be seen piled up besides the workings waiting to be processed. After being extracted, the copper ore was first broken up into smaller pieces, washed, and roasted in kilns. One of the by-products of this process was brimstone, or sulphur.

A third method of extraction, introduced by Medley, was the precipitation process. This consisted of pumping water up the hill to flood the underground workings of an old mine. The copper sulphide would then combine with the oxygen in the water to form copper sulphate, which becomes soluble in water. The resultant solution was then drawn off and run into ponds, into which scrap iron had been thrown. A chemical change then took place as the iron went into the solution, and the copper came out in a fine crystalline powder form. The iron suphate, which became unstable in air, deposited a hydrated oxide of iron which as yellow ochre, was collected and used in the making of paint. Over the years, the streams entering Amlwch have been heavily charged with a deep yellow deposit which can still be seen today on the quay walls and the rocks around the harbour.

Sir Nicholas Bayley, the Rev. Edward Hughes and Thomas Williams formed the Parys Mine Company in 1778. Sir Nicholas belonged to a well-known Anglesey family, and was the grandfather of the first Marquis of Anglesey who we shall meet in the next chapter. Thomas Williams was a solicitor who practised from Beaumaris and was also an entrepreneur and son of a local farmer. He went on to become known as the 'Copper King,' and built up and controlled the vast British Copper Industry which included taking charge of the Cornish mines in the late 1780's, and establishing the copper trade in Abertawe (Swansea), in south Wales.

Eventually, after thirty-two years, Sir Nicholas Bayley leased his share of the land mined by the Parys Mine Company. His son, Henry Paget, who later became the first Earl of Uxbridge formed the Mona Mine Company in 1785, and Thomas Williams, became a partner in the firm with a quarter share.

Smelting in Anglesey began on a large scale, and by the beginning of the 19th century, twenty furnaces were at work at Amlwch alone. The by-products of the mines, which included arsenic, alum, quartz, ochre, sulphur, lead, silver and zinc, brought more work to the area. By 1785, the mines were supplying the navies of Britain, France, Holland, and Spain with copper bolts, nails and copper sheathing. Large shipbuilding companies like the East India Company were placing orders too. At their peak in 1787 the Parys mines consumed one thousand tons of coal a day, at which point the local coal mines could not meet the demand. Consequently coal had to be imported into Anglesey.

Thomas Pennant, the naturalist, antiquary and traveller visited Angelsey in 1778 and his description of the mines in operation provides us with a vivid picture. 'Suffocating fumes issue from the burning heaps of copper, and extend their baneful influence for miles around. In the adjacent parts vegetation is nearly destroyed; even the mosses and lichens of the rocks have perished.' He goes on to say that fifteen hundred people were employed at the mines with some eight thousand people in Anglesey dependent on the mines and their by-products for a living. Miners from other parts of Wales and Cornwall had also been attracted to the area.

The workers operated under dreadful conditions and were lowered on ropes to hack and blast out the rocks as best they could. The average wage was fourpence a day, and in its heyday, although men, women and children worked in the deep opencast mines, little regard was paid to health and safety. The women who worked in these mines were known as *Leeds copper*, copper ladies. They are featured in a well known water colour by J C Iberian, which can be seen in the National Museum of Wales in Cardiff.

In 1786, the then Managing Director of the Parys Mine Company, Thomas Williams, decided to issue his workers with copper trade tokens, which were produced between 1787 and 1793. Richard Collins of Greenwich prepared the original design and the die engraver was John Milton of Fetter Lane, who had also worked in the Tower mint. These minted penny and half penny coins were literally worth their weight in copper. The coins, which soon became collectors items because of their exceptional quality, bore a druid's head within a wreath of oak-leaves and acorns on the obverse. The scrolled letters of Pico, and the date and words 'We promise to pay the bearer,' on the reverse. Indented into the edge of the coins were the words,' on demand in London, Liverpool and Anglesey'. The Anglesey Penny became Thomas Williams supreme symbol and he used it as a seal on all letters pertaining to Mynydd Parys.

Over two hundred different varieties of the coin were made, including proof tokens minted in silver, tin, and copper gilt. The die differences varied greatly, and these were ranged from the number of acorns in wreath type styles, to the smile on the druid's face, which can cause a few headaches for those who catalogue these items for the token collector.

In 1793 Amlwch Harbour, which was once a mere slit in the rocky coast was enlarged in order to accommodate the numerous vessels required to ship the forty-four thousand tons of pure copper produced per year from Anglesey. At the height of production, about forty vessels could be seen anchored in the bay. Copper was loaded onto the ships for the outward journey, and they would return with holds laden with tobacco leaf, which was then processed in factories in Amlwch. With so much activity centred around the town, numerous public houses grew up around the port with the seamen, shipwrights and casual workers all drinking Greenalls beer which was brewed from 1786.

Thanks to the importance of the copper industry, a thriving shipbuilding industry also began to grow on either side of the port. The Treweek family, Captain William Thomas and the Paynter Company built most of the vessels, and there was also a close link between the Amlwch shipbuilders and the Millon iron works in Cumbria. A number of Captain Thomas' workers moved to Cumbria and established a Welsh chapel and community there.

For a while the copper mines of Anglesey and Cornwall were in keen competition, and between them dominated the world market. Soon a 'copper war' broke out, with each trying to undersell the other. This went on until the war with France began, and the market became swamped. Finally, with the death of Thomas Williams in 1801 and the decline in production of the Anglesey mines, the importance of Mynydd Parys waned. Just as demand had risen with the onset of war, so the conclusion of the Napoleonic wars contributed to the decline in the value of copper.

By 1815, due to much undercutting by the Americans and the Africans, the copper trade collapsed. The great days were over, and Amlwch became a ghost town. There was a short-lived revival in 1825, and a brief rise in price increased the prosperity of the Mona Mine Company, but both these events were insufficient to revive an ailing industry. A further revival in the 1830's did not help either, and although a few mines struggled on, none were of any importance after 1850, and by the end of the century the mountain was abandoned.

Today Amlwch is one of the larger towns on Anglesey with a market held every Friday. The area's sea-faring traditions are not forgotten and are reflected in the Catholic Church, Our Lady Star of the Sea and St Winifred. It was built in the 1930's of reinforced concrete, and in the shape of an overturned keel of a boat, complete with portholes!

Amlwch is home to a large secondary School, Ysgol Syr Thomas Jones, which was one of the first purpose built comprehensive schools in the country. Visitors may also be interested to visit the tower of St Eleth's Church, opposite the Dinorben Arms Hotel in Queen Street. This tower was given to the town around 1800 by the Parys Mountain Company and was designed by the architect James Wyatt. At this time he was rebuilding

Plas Newydd, on the south side of the island and which we shall visit in the next chapter.

Between 1973 and 1987, Amlwch became the home of the oil industry. Shell UK operated an offshore terminal, and here tankers of over half a million tonnes could discharge their crude oil, which was then piped to Stanlow in Cheshire, some one hundred and twenty five kilometres away.

But undoubtedly the most picturesque part of the town, and well worth a visit, is the little harbour of Porth Amlwch. In a tranquil setting, trawlers and yachts still moor here alongside a deep quay and an old sail loft, and the 'olde worlde' appearance of its heyday is still in evidence.

CHAPTER SEVENTEEN

PLAS NEWYDD
AND THE FAMILY WHO LIVED THERE

Anyone visiting Ynys Môn should allow at least a couple of hours to visit Plas Newydd, which is situated on the A4080, south of Llanfair Pwllgwyngyll. This magnificent mansion with one hundred and sixty one acres of gardens, parks and woodlands, which border the Menai Straits, was given to the National Trust by the Marquis of Anglesey. It was opened to the public for the first time in 1976 and can be visited between April and September, except on Saturdays. The best time to visit the gardens is in May and June when the azaleas and camellias are at their best.

The Griffith family built the original house, as well as one at Penrhyn near Bangor, in the early 16th century. Since then it has been handed down the generations. As we have seen, the Griffith family were one of the first powerful families in north Wales to emerge as owners of large landed estates. It appears that some of the Môn properties came to Gwilym ap Gruffudd, who died in 1451, through his marriage to Morfydd, daughter of Goronwy ap Tudur of Penmynydd. Morfydd's uncle was the great-grandfather of Henry VII. Gwilym's grandson, Robert, also appears to have been the ancestor of Ellen Griffith of Penrhyn who married Sir Nicholas Bagenal in 1553. He then added this estate to his estates in Ireland, and was appointed Queen Elizabeth's marshal of the army in Ireland, a post which passed to his son Sir Henry.

In the next generation Sir Henry's daughter, Ann, who died in about 1623, married Lewis Bayly who later became the Bishop of Caernarfonshire, and wrote the book The Practice of Piety. It was claimed that Bunyan attributed his book to his spiritual experience. Bishop Bayly also acted as a chaplain to Charles I.

His son, Nicholas Bayly of Plas Newydd, was Governor of Galway and the Isles of Arran as well as gentleman of the Bedchamber to Charles II. In 1730 his son, Edward, was created a baronet, and his son, Sir Nicholas Bayly, married Miss Caroline Paget, great-great-great-great granddaughter of Willam, First Baron Paget de Beaudesert in Staffordshire. Between 1751 and 1753 Sir Nicholas Bayly, added a semicircular turret in the east front of the original building, and an octagonal tower to the south-east corner. It was these two additions in the

Gothic style, which was to dictate the style and unusual plan of the present house.

Sir Nicholas's son, Henry, inherited, through his mother, the title of Lord Paget of Beaudesert and took the name Paget upon succeeding to the barony of Beaudesert in 1769. In 1784, two years after he had inherited Plas Newydd, he was created Earl of Uxbridge. He was largely responsible for consolidating the social and political status for the family in Môn. He also set about altering the house in two distinct stages, believed to have been possible through the vast profits of the Mynydd Parys mine and other ventures.

The first phase of work began in 1783-86 when the mason, John Cooper, built a second octagonal tower at the northern end of the west front to make the house symmetrical. The rooms behind this façade were also substantially remodelled. The second phase of work, between 1795-99, was undertaken by James Wyatt and Joseph Potter of Lichfield who, between them, built a new entrance front on the west side, and created all the Classical and Gothic interiors of the present main block. They also built the castellated stable block, which looks like a three storey house with Tudor caps on slender octagonal turrets. Potter also added the north wing, with an elaborate Chapel on the first floor, between 1805 and 1809, and continued to be employed on farm buildings and lesser alterations to the house into the 1820's. Humphrey Repton, the famous landscape designer was consulted on the layout of the park and gardens, producing one of his famous 'Red Books' for Plas Newydd in 1799. Some of the beech, oak and sycamore trees date back to this time and have flourished in the damp climate near the Straits.

After the death of Lord Uxbridge on 13 March 1812, the estate passed to his eldest son, Field-Marshal Henry William (Bayly) Paget. The 2nd Earl of Uxbridge was created the First Marquis of Anglesey on 4 July three years later for his skill and ability on the field at Waterloo.

The house remained unchanged until 1900 when the Chapel was converted by the Fifth Marquis into a private theatre with its red plush seating and potted palms. During the 1930's the Sixth Marquis removed the battlements from the parapets around the house and altered the sash windows. He also remodelled the north wing, destroyed the chapel-theatre, and created a long ground floor dining room.

Rex Whistler, a close friend of the Paget family, decorated this room between 1936 and 1940. A number of portraits of the family, by Whistler can be seen in this room, as well as a selection of his work as a book illustrator, stage designer and decorative artist. These have kindly been loaned by his younger brother, Laurence Whistler, the poet and glass engraver.

Plas Newydd also contains a small cavalry museum devoted to the campaign relics of the First Marquis of Anglesey, including his famous wooden leg! Henry William Paget was born on 17 May 1768 and became a soldier-statesman. At twenty-two he entered parliament, and three years later he formed the 80th Regiment of Foot. In 1794, under the Duke of Wellington, he fought with the regiment in Flanders, and in 1797 became lieutenant colonel of the 7th Light Dragoons (later Hussars). It was under his command that the regiment became one of the finest cavalry units in the army. His first actions were fought in the Netherlands in 1799, and by the time he went to Portugal in 1808, he had became a lieutenant general. At this time his private life became complicated, when he eloped with the Duke of Wellington's sister-in-law. After costly divorce proceedings they married in 1810 and had ten children.

In 1815 he was appointed commander of the allied cavalry in the Netherlands – second in command to Wellington. His retreat through Genappe on 17th June, and his handling of the cavalry at Waterloo the following day, earned him a lasting place in history. Whilst riding across the battlefield with the victorious Duke at the end of the day, grapeshot shattered his right leg. It is claimed that he cried, 'By God, sir, I've lost my leg!' Wellington apparently lowered his telescope and responded, 'By God sir, so you have!', before immediately raising his telescope to his eye and continuing to watch the French in flight. Later that day, without anaesthetic, the commander's leg was amputated and buried under a small monument in a garden at Waterloo. George Canning, the statesman, is reputed to have written its epitaph:

'Here rests – and let no saucy knave
Presume to sneer and laugh,
To learn that mouldering in this grave
There lies a British calf.

For he who writes these lines is sire
That those who read the whole
Will find that laugh was premature
For here, too, lies the sole.

Three weeks later in London, the Prince Regent (later George IV) rewarded him with the title of First Marquis of Angelsey and declared that he was his best officer and his best subject.

Some years later he was given a wooden leg, one of the first articulated artificial limbs to be designed by the famous James Potts, of Chelsea, This was patented as the 'Anglesey Leg' and was still being advertised as such as late as 1914.

The Marquis, known as 'One Leg' lived to be eighty-six years, and fathered a total of eighteen children and had seventy-three grandchildren! His family papers and personal correspondence shows that he gave his support to every cause and movement of importance on Ynys Môn.

In 1816, the villagers opened a subscription for an 'eligible memorial'. Within a week over eight hundred and sixty pounds was raised. The proceeds were used to erect a one hundred foot (thirty metre) column of distinctive Anglesey grey marble (called Doric), which had been brought from Moelfre. It was designed by Thomas Harrison, and stands on a knoll, two hundred and fifty feet (seventy six metres) above the sea and can be reached through a field just outside the village of Llanfair Pwllgwyngyll. Its long inscription recalls the Marquis's distinguished military achievement in the Peninsula War, and the unforgettable Battle of Waterloo.

Forty-three years later in 1860, the sculptor Matthew Noble designed a twelve foot (three and a half metre) bronze of the Marquis as colonel of the 7th Hussars, with the Order of the Bath and Waterloo Medal to be placed on top of the column. The plume of his shako, his military head-dress, reaches three hundred and sixty feet (one hundred and ten metres) above the Menai Straits and commands, a magnificent view of the whole area.

The erection of this bronze demanded a major operation. The statute, weighing between two and three tons, was hoisted and positioned through an intricate system of scaffolding and pulleys devised by a Mr Haslam of Carreg-brân, nearby. The feat is illustrated on a copper engraving fixed to the statues pedestal. Despite local belief, the statue does not show the Marquis complete with his 'Anglesey Leg'.

Another interesting member of the family was the Fifth Marquis of Anglesey, known to his friends as 'Toppy'. He loved the theatre, hence the reason why he turned the Chapel into a theatre and engaged all the best companies in London. He loved playing the main parts himself, and had himself portrayed on picture postcards decked in pearl and diamond-studded costumes, a sort of David Garrick of Plas Newydd. In the winter months he used to have little stoves dotted along the forest paths so that he could warm himself when out walking. He died when only thirty years old, and was succeeded by his cousin who had no time for his theatre. He demolished it and put in a new dining room, with guest rooms above, each with a bathroom. The Sixth Marquis had a love of the art of illusion and this can be seen on the walls of the dining room, created by a series of trompe-l'oeil fantasies by Rex Whistler. Within these magical landscapes can been seen castles in the air, and a Renaissance town in the southern sun. There are also illusion pictures on both sides of the central painting, giving the appearance of rooms leading off into colonnades. In one of these can be seen a book and a pair of spectacles belonging to Lady Anglesey; her daughter's dogs; and her son's cello.

The present Marquis is a founder member of the Historic Buildings Council for Wales, and is a keen military historian. He is currently writing a history of the British Cavalry.

CHAPTER EIGHTEEN

SOME FAMOUS AND NOT SO FAMOUS PEOPLE

Môn, like all places in Wales, has its fair share of notable sons and daughters, and to mention them all would require a whole book. Some, such as the Tudur family, the Bulkeleys' of Beaumaris, and the Marquis's of Anglesey, we have met.

One of the most accomplished Welsh families of their time were the Morris family (widely known as Morysiaid Môn). Brothers, Lewis, Richard and William, had a tremendous effect on the cultural history of Wales, as well as joining the two greatest movements of the 18th century – the classical and popular.

They were born during the early eighteenth century at either Y Fferam or Tyddyn-melys, in the beautifully named parish of Llanfihangel Tre'r-beirdd, and were brought up at Pentre-eiriannell at Penrhosllugwy. Sadly the stone building in which they were born is now simply an outhouse of the present farmhouse and no lasting memorial or plaque records their importance at their birth-place. They belonged to the gwerin, the common people of Wales, and their father, Morys ap Rhisiart Morys, was a carpenter and cooper. However, they were aware that they were descended from the old aristocratic family of Bulkeley although Lewis Morris, the most famous of the three, claimed he had little formal education.

Lewis (1701-1765) learnt his father's craft, but from a very young age he took an interest in Welsh Literature and in old manuscripts. From 1729 to 1743 he held the post of surveyor of taxes in Beaumaris and Holyhead. During those years he also carried out land surveying work for the Admiralty, and was given the task of making a map of the Welsh coast.

In 1746 he became an official for the crown lands of Cardiganshire and attempted to control the search for lead and silver in the county. This was met with bitter controversy by some of the minor squires who on one occasion succeeded in getting him thrown into prison.

He is remembered for many reasons – as an antiquarian, prose-writer, mineralogist, surveyor and engineer, but chiefly as a poet and a man of letters. The letters the brother wrote to each other give us a detailed account of social conditions in Môn. Lewis also wrote many poems in 'free' metre as well as in 'strict' metre, and had a talent for humorous verse. He collected valuable Welsh manuscripts, and brought to the attention of others the treasures that lay hidden in old manuscripts. He copied some of them himself and, in 1735, he set up a printing press in

Holyhead to publish Welsh books. Sadly this venture was not a success, and only two numbers of a journal, Tlysau yr Hen Oesoedd (Treasures of Ancient Times) were ever published.

It was near the town of Holyhead that a strange phenomenon occurred sometime in 1743. Lewis Morris, now an experienced mining engineer, had a report from a Mr William John Lewis, a farmer from nearby Peibio. It read:

'Plowing with his servant in ye fields, he saw bearing down upon him a ship of ninety tons, rigged like a ketch, with its fore-tack at the cathead and its pennant and 'antient' flying. The day was described as indifferent and cloudy, but the detail of the ship could be clearly seen, it was coming from yea mountains of Snowdon, not by sailing of the waves around Holy island, but moving about a quarter of a mile high from ye ground. The farmer called his wife. She ran from the farmhouse in time to see the ship in the sky retreating, its pennant lowered to the deck and all sails furled. It was steering 'stern foremast' making for whence it had come, the mountains of Snowdon.'

Lewis Morris rushed off to Holyhead and firstly interviewed the wife. Although she had no idea of the sea terms she described clearly, and with no hesitation, what she had seen. Her only concern was what her neighbours would think if anything relating to the event was ever published. Lewis Morris then interviewed her husband who explained that the ship had been easy to see, exact in every detail, and even the keel could be seen from below. He also claimed that the ropes of the rigging were so clear that they were able to count each, one by one. The sails were cumbersome with the wind, and the foresail lowered. The farmer had watched until, finally, a cloud hid the vessel. The farmer, his wife and a young lad also reported that they had seen a flock of birds' hover above the ship and had flown around it in all directions. They also observed that when the vessel began its return journey, the birds had flown from it northwards in the opposite direction.

The farmer assured Lewis Morris that he had seen another such ship in exactly the same place ten years before, and another, ten years before that. By the description, each ship had been very much like the packet-boats that plied the sea between Holyhead and Ireland.

Lewis Morris interpreted this series of phenomena as a sign of some great disaster, and tried unsuccessful,y to find a link with the ten-year intervals. For the cynics, the explanation may lie in the fact that the hill at Holyhead is the only height in Môn to face the distant elevations of

Snowdonia. Perhaps by some trick of refraction the mountain may have picked up an image of the vessels plying the Menai Straits, and set them to steer the skies above Peibio. Or perhaps there was some other strange reason for the ghost ship?

In 1751, Richard Morris established a society in London, Anrhydeddus Gymdeithas y Cymmrodorion (the Honourable Society of Cymmrodorion). He saw this as an academy on similar lines to the French Academy or the Royal Society, and drew up long lists of subjects for study and debate. The brothers attended several meetings in London and, although Lewis was disappointed with them, he continued to send learned papers to be read at the meetings. Sadly, the only works published in Lewis Morris' lifetime were his poems, but there are many volumes of his manuscripts in the British Museum and in the National Library of Wales.

Lewis died in 1765 and was buried at Llanbadarn Fawr near Aberystwyth. A Celtic Cross, a fitting memorial to Morysiaid Môn, stands on a hill overlooking the A5025, halfway between Benllech and Amlwch, and just a few yards north of Brynrefail.

Not far from here, a mile to the west of Benllech, is the isolated church of Llanfair Mathafarn Eithaf. It is in a cottage in this parish that another Anglesey figure, Goronwy Owen, was born in 1723. He became a friend of the Morris brothers. He was one of three children of a very poor family and was encouraged and inspired by the Morris brothers and, through the help of Lewis, was educated in classics at Friars' School in Bangor. He entered Jesus College, Oxford as a server but spent little time there. Although he was an excellent Greek and Latin scholar he did not take a degree; but later in life became one of the leaders of the classical renaissance in Wales. All Goronwy wanted from life was a Welsh curacy, and to write poetry. After Oxford he worked for a short time as a curate in his native parish and wrote his poetry which, unfortunately, was not published until forty years after his death. A permanent curacy eluded him and he moved from one ill-paid parish to another. We are not sure why he did not obtain a curacy, but he was known to drink too much, and was scorned by most of his peers. Finally he found a post as a grammar school master at the William and Mary College, Williamsburg, Virginia, at a salary of two hundred pounds.

Sadly his wife and baby son died on the journey to America, and although we know very little of his life there, we do know that from Williamsburg he accepted a post at St Andrews, Brunswick County and then bought a plantation and grew tobacco and cotton. He married two more times, died in 1769, and is buried on his plantation. He left a cow and yearling, a gray horse, four Negro slaves as well as two sermons when he died.

Welsh exiles from all over the world joined together and contributed to a pulpit, which was installed in the church at Llanfair Mathafarn Eithaf on the bi-centenary of his death. There is also a marble tablet in his memory at Bangor Cathedral.

Although he was a difficult man who died in exile in America, he never forgot his love for Môn. He had studied all the great poets, Homer, Virgil, and Pope and had taken many of the fifteenth century Welsh poets as his role model. One of his poems, which highlights the destruction of the world by fire, also shows that he is thinking of his beloved Môn:

When Anglesey with its gentleness
From the flames's heat will be one scorching
Its pregnant veins of silver
Its lead and steel one flame of fire.

George Borrow outlines the tale of Goronwy Owen in his book Wild Wales, and said:

he was one of the last of the great poets of Cambria, and the exception of Dafydd ab Gwilym, the greatest she(Cambria) has produced.

When Borrow visited Môn he went to great lengths to seek out Goronwy's birthplace and, as a memento of his visit, he took away some leaves from a sycamore tree, which grew near the house.

Another great Môn man was Sir Hugh Owen (1804-1881) who was knighted in recognition for his services to Welsh education. He was born in a farmhouse called Y Foel, which stands on the shores of the Menai Straits between Talyfoel and Brynsiencyn. He found work in London and took part in many important religious and social movements in the capital. He was instrumental in re-starting the Anrhydeddus Gymdeithas y Cymmrodorion in 1873, and worked hard to bring about many reforms to the National Eisteddfod.

Though he became well known in many fields, Sir Hugh's greatest achievements were in the field of Welsh education. His Llythyr at y Cymry in 1843 proved to be instrumental in establishing non-denominational schools for the children of Wales. He was also a key figure in establishing colleges for the training of teachers in Wales, and it is thanks to his efforts that the University College of Wales at Aberystwyth was established and maintained.

Another man, the grand old man of Tregalen, must surely earn a place amongst the less famous of Anglesey. When William ap Howell ap Howell ap Dafydd ap Iowerth died on March 11 1581 at Tregalen near Llangefi, he had reached the grand age of 105. It is claimed that some three hundred of the congregation who attended his funeral were descended from him. William's first wife produced twenty-two children, his second, Katherine, a further ten, and this third wife, Elin, four. It is also claimed that he fathered seven children out of wedlock! By the time his youngest son, Gruffudd was born, his eldest son, also called Gruffudd, was almost eighty-two years of age. William rarely suffered from illness and lived the life of a countryman, enjoying fishing and fowling and enjoying a meagre diet that consisted mainly of goat's milk. Obviously his lifestyle suited his constitution!

During the eighteenth century, Niwbwrch (Newborough) became the centre of a lawsuit, involving an English clergymen who, although not a true son of Môn, should earn a place amongst the not-so-well-known or infamous. It began when the Bishop of Bangor, following the general custom of appointing English Clergymen to the best Welsh parishes, appointed seventy-two year old Dr Bowles to Trefdraith. The Doctor could not speak a word of Welsh, and tried preaching to his congregation of two hundred and fifty Welsh speakers in English.

At the time there was a law in Wales, which was not too readily enforced, stating that divine service should take place in the

'vernacular language of Wales, with fluent and easy delivery, and a graceful propriety of accent and pronunciation.'

The Doctor tried to cope with the aid of a Welsh prayer book and a Welsh Bible, and no doubt a few silent prayers! Unfortunately his accent and pronunciation let him down, and his congregation were so disgusted that they walked out of his services!

An action was started to get rid of Bowles, and the case came before the Court of Arches. The parson presented the court with a certificate stating that his Welsh was perfect. It had been signed, as the law required, by two churchwardens and one other parishioner. It transpired that one of the church wardens was none other that his own son-in-law. The other, the local shoemaker, had made the parson a pair of shoes and thought that he was signing a receipt for the money he had received! The third, a man called Richard Williams, was not asked to read the document but accepted the fact that, because two other men had signed it, he should do likewise.

The case lasted three years and Dr Bowles actually won. By now he was seventy-five and the people of Trefdraith claimed that they were like a flock of sheep without a shepherd. Others jibed that, although they were able to say they had a shepherd, they were unable to understand the sound of the shepherd's voice.

Last, but certainly not least, we should remember the cleverness and devotion of Tyger. Tyger, was not a famous man, but a very special dog who saved the lives of his master, two men, and a boy, after their ship had come to grief off the coast of the island.

It all began on the night of 17 September 1819. A ketch, bound for Liverpool, became stuck on the dangerous Maen Piscar (rock) and almost immediately began to sink. The fog, which had lasted for about three days, was so thick that the four on board could not see the coastline, and did not know which way to swim to safety. The captain had a vague idea of his whereabouts, but Tyger, the captains retriever, barked eagerly as he, at any rate, knew which way the land lay. The ketch began to sink, and Tyger, with the ship's boy clinging to his collar, began to swim. The captain, trusting the dog's instinct, followed. Tyger struggled for a quarter of a mile, through the surf to reach safety. Although extremely tired the dog returned to his master and the two others. One of the men was in difficulties, and lagging behind the other two. Tyger swam out and tugged the seaman ashore by the collar of his jacket.

All four managed to reach safety, although in a state of complete exhaustion. But sadly the strain had been too much for Tyger and, as he feebly licked his master's hand, he died in his arms. His broken-hearted master buried him in the south-eastern corner of Penrhos bay, on the cliff-top over the Black Arch. A two foot high memorial stone marks the grave, and was erected with the simple inscription:

'Tyger, September 17th 1819.'

Perhaps readers would also be interested in not a famous person, but a very strange coincidence of name and date. On December 5 1664, a boat was crossing the Menai Straits with eighty-one passengers on board when it was hit by a gale. The only survivor was a man named Hugh Williams. More than one hundred years later, on December 5 1780, another vessel with a large number of passengers came to grief. There were few survivors but once again, a man called Hugh Williams was saved. On December 5 1820, a boat laden with thirty people sank on the same spot, and yes, you have guessed correctly; the sole survivor was a man called Hugh Williams!

CHAPTER NINETEEN

VICTORIAN ANGLESEY
AND
THE TELFORD AND BRITANNIA BRIDGES

Although the copper mines, and the prospect of higher wages attracted many to Amlwch, farming still continued to dominate the rest of the economy of Môn. It was therefore obvious that when the copper industry began to decline, the islanders looked towards the old traditions of the land and cattle farming to see them through the lean years.

As you can imagine Môn's abundant supply of corn also gave rise to a flourishing milling industry. Both wind and water powered these, and the results can still be seen today, dotted all over the island. Unfortunately few water mills survive, but many of the tall windmill towers remain, although some have now been converted into homes.

In 1929 the Royal Commission reporting on Ancient Monuments said that thirty-seven 18th and 19th century windmills were found, and that some still possessed their sails. One, Melin Llynon at Llanddeusant, has been restored by Anglesey Borough Council and is now the only working windmill in Wales. Melin Llynon was built in 1775-6 for Herbert Jones, and suffered severe storm damage in 1918, and fell out of use in the 1920's. The county council bought it in 1978, and restoration work began using the original internal workings, although new woodwork was needed. It was finally opened to the public in May 1984 and is visited by over twelve thousand five hundred people every year. The three pairs of millstones and hoists were restored, and now work to grind flour.

The water that surrounds Môn also played its part in the expansion of the area, especially in its connections with Ireland. From the 17th century records that survive, we find that the main reason people came to Môn was to cross over to Ireland on the regular Holyhead packet boat service. However, by the middle of the 18th century the growth of northern cities like Manchester and Liverpool, and also of Dublin in Ireland, meant that people were turning more to London for commerce. So it is hardly surprising to learn that by the end of the 18th century various proposals were put forward to build a bridge across the Menai Strait in order to improve communications between Dublin and London. There had been an Old Horse Ferry in operation across the Menai Straits since the 13th century, originally shared between the crown and the town of

Porthaethwy (Menai Bridge). In 1502 it became the sole property of the crown before falling into private hands.

The need for a bridge across the Strait was obvious but it took rather a long time for the idea to catch on. There was a presentation of a Bill in Parliament as early as 1786 but all the early attempts failed. However, any visitor to Ynys Môn cannot fail today to be impressed by the sight of not one, but two excellent 19th century building wonders of north Wales – Telford's Suspension Bridge and Stephenson's Tubular Bridge. They stand as proud monuments of human effort, enterprise, industry and a good degree of faith based on pure genius.

Pont y Borth (the Menai Strait Suspension Bridge) must have been photographed from every conceivable angle, and appears in every guidebook, as well as on commemorative plates and cups. It even once featured on banknotes. In the wind it swings gently like a giant hammock. The Britannia Bridge, reminds the onlooker of a giant rabbit hole with the train disappearing through one of two rectangular tubes, one hundred feet (thirty metres) above the water, and emerging on the other side. It seems a fitting memorial that as these two bridges stand side by side over the Menai Straits, the bodies of their builders, Stephenson and Telford, rest side by side in Westminster Abbey.

Perhaps before we learn more about the bridges we should pay a visit to Porthaethwy (Menai Bridge) town. The centre of the town contains shops, offices, restaurants, and Victorian houses which were once the homes of the affluent shipowners of the era. The narrow streets lead down to the water front and, until the bridge was built, this was the site of the ferry. The timber yard, situated opposite the Liverpool Arms has been in use from about 1828. It was owned by the Davies family of Treborth whose ships were responsible for exporting slates, and also carried many emigrants away from the poverty of Wales. The timber provided the ballast for the return voyages. During the early 19th century paddle steamers from Liverpool moored at St George's Pier, now much shorter than it was in those days. Today the research vessel, Prince Madog, owned by Bangor University's School of Ocean Sciences, is moored here. This is one of the leading study centres in the United Kingdom. The Tourist Information Centre is to the left of the A5, past the first roundabout, and is a good source for information of the many attractions in the area. If you have a few minutes to spare, take a walk along Belgian Walk, along the west promenade. During the War, the Belgian refugees stationed in the area constructed this Walk.

It was not until John Rennie and Captain Joseph Huddart arrived, in 1801, to study the problems of bridging the Menai Straits that the idea of building a bridge finally became a possibility. Rennie produced a design which consisted of a series of cast-iron arches, but it never got built, probably because of the expense.

It was also found that the road between Holyhead and Shrewsbury was, according to a contemporary report, 'a miserable tract composed of a succession of circuitois and craggy ineqaluties.' Thomas Telford was asked to examine the route between Shrewsbury and Holyhead and proposed the possibility of a road through Capel Curig, Llyn Ogwen and the Nant Ffrancon pass. Telford was the son of a Scottish shepherd and qualified as a stone mason before teaching himself engineering. In 1801 he had proposed that the new London Bridge should consist of a single cast iron arch, spanning some six hundred and sixty feet (two hundred metres). This was met with opposition as people considered it far too daring. However, his idea for a road linking Holyhead and Shrewsbury caught on, and he was commissioned by the government to build the Holyhead Turnpike Road – the modern day A5. Before the road was built travellers faced a nightmare journey along narrow roads, with a maximum speed of seven and a half miles per hour, and run the risk of journeys being delayed in wet weather when carriage wheels became stuck in the mud. Telford built a road that not only improved the comfort of the passengers, but also helped to raise the commercial traffic to and from Ireland. Its only drawback was its expense and it had to be financed by a series of tollgates, which Telford designed. One of the last four remaining early octagonal tollgates and houses on Ynys Môn can be seen today at Llanfairpwll Pwllgwyngyll. On the building is the original table of tolls which ceased on 1 November 1895, by which time this was the only public toll road in the United Kingdom. Two other examples, distinctive by their octagonal fronts, can be seen at Gwalchmai and Caergeiliog. Attached to the toll house at Llanfairpwll Pwllgwyngyll is a corrugated iron building which was erected in 1921, and just one hundred yards (ninety-one metres) from here, the first ever meeting of the Women's Institute took place in 1915. The movement, which was introduced from Canada by a connection with a Môn family, remains popular in the area today, with this particular local branch still going strong.

The only missing link between London and Ireland was the spanning of the Menai Straits. The matter of bridging the Straits was considered again, and Rennie's scheme was almost adopted. However, at about this time, Telford who had been commissioned by the Treasury to survey the whole road system in north Wales, was considering the possibility of suspension, by wrought iron cables, as an alternative to the favoured arched method of bridging. In 1817 he produced a plan for such a bridge at Runcorn in Cheshire. The following year he submitted a design to the committee of the House of Commons, for a suspension bridge across the Menai Straits, which was immediately approved. The first stone was laid at noon on Tuesday 10 August 1820 by Mr Provis, a resident engineer. The bridge, the first big iron one in the world, has a main span of five hundred and seventy-nine feet (one hundred and seventy-six metres), suspended from two limestone pillars on wrought iron chains, one hundred feet (ninety-one metres) above the level of the water at high tide. This was to meet Admiralty Navigation requirements, so that the tall ships could pass under in safety. Telford had each of the sixteen chains meticulously tested for tension many times before he was ready to float them on a giant raft into position between the pylons. The first twenty-three ton cable was hoisted into place by means of a pulley system, whilst one hundred and fifty men were kept in time by a fife band! They celebrated their achievement by running across the nine-inch-wide chain from Anglesey to the mainland! It is amazing to think, in our safety conscious environment, that this entire bridge was assembled without scaffolding, and that only four fatalities occurred during its erection – ironically an Englishman, An Irishman, A Scotsman and a Welshman!

Near the Anglesey shore is a low rock on which stands the Western pier of the bridge. This is known as Ynys-y-moch because in the old days, animals had to swim across the strait to get to market. This was done in two stages to allow the pigs to rest on this island. When the suspension bridge was built the current owner of the ferry service, Miss Williams, was paid compensation of £26,934 for the loss of dues estimated to be nine hundred pounds per annum.

On January 26 1826 the first post-chaise crossed the bridge as onlookers clapped and cheered; a truly momentous day for the people of Môn. The official general opening of the bridge took place on Monday 30 January, when the Royal London and Holyhead mail coach, carrying the London mail-bag for Dublin, passed over at 1 a.m. Not only did this bridge allow for better communications, but also for the starting up of the tourist trade.

In 1938 the bridge was strengthened to take the increased traffic. The work involved replacing the original chains with stronger ones, and replacing the double carriageway with a singe broad carriageway with outside walkways for foot passengers. The work was completed by 1941, and about this time the toll to cross the bridge was discontinued. The museum at Bangor had a fine display relating to the construction of the bridge, including some of Telfords original drawings and prints, Telford's chair from the Castle Hotel Bangor, and part of one of the original links.

The impressive Britannia Railway Bridge, which takes its name from the rock supporting the central pier, was built by Robert Stephenson, the son of the famous railway pioneer, George Stephenson. Work began in 1846 to the west of the Telford structure, but it was not until 1850 that the first London to Holyhead express train ran across the Straits. The bridge consisted of two huge tubes, supported on three massive stone towers, one hundred feet (ninety-one metres) above the water, and guarded at each end by two stone lions, thirteen feet (four metres) high and twenty-five feet (eight metres) wide. The total length of the bridge, including the approaches, measures about one third of a mile (five hundred and thirty-three metres). Construction began on the railway track between Holyhead and Chester on St David's Day 1845. Three years later the station at Llanfairpwll Pwllgwyngyll was opened when two locomotives were shipped to Holyhead. Today, next to the old station house, stands the large John Pringle Weavers shop which has a superb range of knitware and clothing. In 1995 the old station house was restored to how it would have looked in Victorian times by James Pringle Weavers, and it is well worth a visit. Here you can relax with a cup of tea and a piece of Bara Brith, the famous speckled Welsh bread, before buying one of the famous platform tickets.

In 1900 the two huge tubes were covered by a timber canopy, which bore a catwalk along the centre to serve as access for maintenance purposes. It was then roofed with pitch soaked canvas. Unfortunately this was to prove disastrous when a major fire broke out on the bridge on 23 May 1970 It appears that two boys, looking for bats on the bridge, ran off when they heard someone calling, and dropped a lighted torch as they went An eye-witness reported that;

'Not only smoke but also large orange flames could be seen issuing furiously from the tops of the tubes of the bridge. It was a beautiful clear evening with a strongish south-westerly wind blowing. As night fell, the wind increased. The flames spread quite quickly to the first stone tower, but it was completely dark by the time they reached the central tower . . . '

When dawn broke, it was found that the paint on the north side of the tubes had been burnt off in some places, but, otherwise, except for the blacking of the tops of the towers, everything looked the same as before. It was decided that the wooden lining of the original bridge should to be replaced by steel, and a series of arches were added to support a road deck over the bridge. In the nearby church, rebuilt in 1853, stands an obelisk at the top of the churchyard commemorating those who died in connection with the building of the bridge: eight men died of injuries; the chief accountant died of typhus fever in his twenty-seventh year, and one Emma Greaves who died at Britannia Bridge in her fifth year. Unfortunately it does not tell us why, or indeed when.

Overlooking the bridge on the Môn side stands the Nelson Monument which was erected in 1873 as a navigational aid, in tribute to the famous admiral, by Admiral the Right Honorable the Earl of Uxbridge, Clarence Paget. On the base of the monument are the words, in English and Welsh, 'Fell at Trafalgar, 1805.'

With the coming of the railway, Holyhead harbour was improved and the West Pier opened in 1858. The inner harbour, together with the railway station and hotel were not completed until 1875, and were officially opened by the then Prince of Wales in 1880. A clock was erected to commemorate the event.

The hub of Victorian Beaumaris was the Green, and the sea-front with its pier where the paddle steamers from Merseyside once docked, bringing the first tourists to Anglesey. Today the Bulkeley Hotel and the imposing frontage of Victoria Terrace dominate the sea front. Edward Welch and Joseph Hansom completed the hotel in 1835, one year after Hansom patented the safety cab, which still bears his name. In the basement of the hotel the visitor will find the Time-Tunnel – an experience that allows the visitor, through static displays and audiovisual presentations, to be transported back to Beaumaris' past.

The circle of standing stones on the Green was the site of the Proclamation, in 1995, of Eisteddfod Môn (the Anglesey regional eisteddfod).

Just above the town of Beaumaris stands the ruin of Barron Hill, home to the Bulkeley family. It was built by Samuel Wyatt (1776), with alterations made in the 19th century by David Moore. The house was partly gutted by fire during the second World War. The park was designed by William Emes, and the Bulkeley Memorial (a tall obelisk) was erected in 1875; it is situated in the fields one mile north west of the house.

Another reminder of the Victorian era is Beaumaris Goal in Steeple Lane, and well worth a visit. This was built by Hansom in 1829 and its design became the model pattern for prisons. Archive material details the history of the prison and prison life, as well as crimes and punishments in Gwynedd from the 16th century. The treadmill in the yard, the only one left in the United Kingdom, reminds the visitor of the miseries and treatments inflicted on the inmates. The women prisoners did the cooking, and were allowed to rock their baby's cradles in the nursery above by means of a pulley system. The visitor can see the cells, including those for condemned prisoners and the first floor walkway which leads through a door in the outer wall to the scaffold. Two prisoners were hanged here. The last, in 1862, was Dic Rowland (Richard Rowlands) who, it is said, cursed the church clock opposite the goal. Although it has never worked well, most believe that this is because it is exposed to the winter gales that hit the island. It is Richard's disembodied voice that the visitor hears at the beginning of the recorded tour of the buildings and display.

CHAPTER TWENTY

SHIPPING, WRECKING AND MYSTERY

When you consider that Ynys Môn is surrounded by sea, it is hardly surprising to learn that it has played a major role in the lives of its inhabitants. Not only have the residents been able to make a good living from the sea, legally by trade or tourism; they have also made a fair living from piracy, smuggling and wrecking.

As far back of 1783, the historian Henry Parry noted that:

'the Druidical Society of Anglesey offered £10 to any farmer on the coast of Anglesey, Caernarfonshire or Merioneth who gave the greatest assistance with men and horses to save life from any vessel wrecked in the neighbourhood.'

This offer annoyed those who had banded themselves into wrecking and smuggling gangs but, thankfully, there were more honest people than the ones who were concerned with plundering.

One of the most dangerous parts of the surrounding sea is around the small islet (off the most northern part of Ynys Môn) called the Skerries. Its Welsh name is Ynysoedd y Moelrhoniaid, which means the isle of seals for obvious reasons. The Skerries was valued in the olden days for its superb fishing grounds, and its importance was such that it was once the subject of a court case. In the 15th century the Skerries belonged to Bangor Cathedral, but when the Griffiths family of Penrhyn put a gwely (a bed) on the island, they claimed that, according to Welsh custom, this gave them ownership of the island as well as the fishing rights. The Bishop of Bangor re-possessed the islands, but one of the Griffith sons reacted,

'with dyvers men in harnes wich ryetwoely in the seid county of Anglesey with the seid bishope's diocese, took the seid fishis from the servants of the seid bishope'.

The Bishop prosecuted them and won the case.

For over two hundred years there has been a light on Skerries Rock to warn unsuspecting vessels of its dangers. This began as a fire of coals burning in a brazier, and evolved into the erection of the modern lighthouse. The lighthouse was founded by William Trench, an Irishman who was born in 1642. In 1713, Trench obtained a ninety-nine year lease for the Skerries from William Robinson of Gwersyllt and Mynachdy. The rent was set at ten pounds per annum until a beacon was built, then for a rent of twenty pounds per year. The following year, Queen Anne granted William a patent which gave him the power to erect a beacon on the Skerries, and to levy a fee of one penny per ton on all shipping passing by, except those engaged in war. On 4 November 1716 the first beacon was lit on the Skerries, but in the years that followed it proved to be an unprofitable venture. William not only didn't recover enough to cover the cost of the maintanance, but he also lost his only son to the sea, when he was taking a cargo of materials to the Skerries. William died in 1725 and the lighthouse passed to his son-in-law, Rev Sutton Morgan.

Five years after he took over, an Act of Parliament was passed which granted him the power to enforce a payment of proper fees, but he died before he could benefit from these new powers. At this time the lighthouse consisted of a round tower, about thirty-five feet (eleven metres) high, on which a fire blazed from an open bucket-shaped grate. This fire had to be continually fuelled, and consumed between eighty and one hundred tons of coal a year. William's interest in the Skerries, which by this time was amounting to a huge sum of eleven hundred pounds per annum, was passed to his niece Rebecca Morgan.

In 1739 William Robinson, the grandson of the William Robinson who had originally leased the Skerries to William Trench, together with twelve of his companions, were drowned as they attempted to return from the rock during a severe storm. The only person to survive the ordeal was a boy who had remained on the Skerries when the boat departed. The party had been drinking heavily, and the boy had tried to stop them leaving, but they were too full of liquor to take any notice of him. They became aggressive and tried to force the boy to leave with them, but he knew the dangers of setting out in a storm. Frightened, he managed to escape from them, and hid under some straw in the stable. Too drunk to know what they were doing, they followed him and grabbed a pitchfork and began to prod the straw. Although the boy was half-suffocating he managed to stay motionless until, finally, the party gave up and set off on their fatal journey without him.

In 1778 Rebecca Morgan died and responsibility for the light passed to her younger sister's son, Morgan Jones. In 1804 he built a new lighthouse which had a lantern containing an oil lamp with reflectors. William Trench's original lease was now drawing to a close and his heir made a new contract with the heirs of the Robinson family. In 1810 Morgan Jones became the owner of the Skerries and when he died in 1826, the ownership passed to his nephew, another Morgan Jones. By the year 1828 the income from the lighthouse had risen to nearly twelve thousand pounds per year. Seven years later Trinity House approached Morgan Jones with a view to purchasing the Skerries, but the offer was turned down as were two further offers, in 1838 for two hundred and sixty thousand pounds, and in 1839 for three hundred thousand pounds. By the following year Trinity House had bought all the private lighthouses except the Skerries, which now had light dues amounting to twenty-three thousand pounds per year, thanks to overseas trade attracted by the Port of Liverpool. When Morgan died he had no heir to inherit his estate. A special jury was therefore convened at Beaumaris Sheriff's Court to settle the financial arrangements. The sum of £444,984.11s 2d was awarded and, after various mortgages and debts had been deducted, the representatives of the late Morgan Jones received two thirds of the money and the descendants of William Robinson one third. The Skerries then became the property of Trinity House, focusing its guiding light on a sea route that was estimated to be worth half a million pounds.

The West Mouse is another rocky islet which stands proud in the area around Trwyn y Gadair (Carmel Head) and the Skerries. It's Welsh name is Maen-y-Bugail (the stone of the shepherd) and derives from an old tale about a shepherd who, on getting a stone in his shoe, took it out and threw it as far as he could, and it landed in the sea.

The West Mouse has also been a scene of disaster. On 26 March 1823, the sailing packet Alert, under the command of Captain Morgan, left Howth bound for Holyhead with passengers and freight. They found themselves becalmed between Carmel Head and the Skerries, leaving the vessel at the mercy of the strong flood tide. The fierce current caught her and she was flung onto the outlying rocks of West Mouse, where she was holed. Only seven people managed to reach the shore alive.

Unfortunately, whenever there are dangerous rocks, there is also a thriving activity amongst the wreckers. Near Rhosneigr, home since the late 1770's of a thriving shipbuilding industry, worked a gang of wreckers called Lladron Grigyll (the Wreckers of Grigyll). The original 'gang' was active as early as 1715, when its members were brought to trial. It is recorded that:

'On Tuesday 25 April, 1715, at the County Goal, Beaumaris, were committed for felony three men, known as Lladron Creigiau Grigyll (The robbers of the Grigyll rocks), who were found guilty of plundering the wreck of the sloop called The Charming Jenny stranded at Grigyll.'

Those were the days of harsh punishments, when even the theft of a loaf of bread was a hanging offence, and although there is no records to prove it, it is very probable that this little band of wreckers met with a sticky end. After the gangs demise, various groups continued to flourish under their name, more particularly during the latter part of the eighteenth century. They became notorious for their activities of luring unsuspecting ships to their doom by holding lanterns above dangerous rock. When the ships hit the rocks they were the first on the scene to plunder them. On 30 November 1867, The Times reported that:

'The wreck (Earl of Chester) is now prey to the notorious wreckers of the coast known to Welsh seafaring men as Lladron Grigyll (the Grigyll robbers). Many hundreds of them were there yesterday stealing whatever they could carry away.'

Another infamous band of Grigyll wreckers who were also caught; Owen John Ambrose of Llanfihangel-yn-Nhywyn, Gabriel Roberts of Caergeiliog, Thomas Roberts and Hugh Griffith Hughes of Llanfaelog, were more fortunate. They were tried in April 1741, at Beaumaris Assizes, before Mr Justice Martyn. All were accused of robbing a Liverpool brigantine, the Loveday & Betty, which had been driven onshore and stranded by the south-westerly gales of 31 December 1740. Once again, the penalty they faced for felony was the noose, and the trial attracted such a lot of attention that many notable businessmen travelled to attend the trial.

Once of these, William Bulkeley, recorded in his diary: 'Though this is the last day of the Sessions, the Court sat to try causes till three in the evening; a thing never known before in the history of man. Martyn, the Judge, being every day drunk, deferred all business to the last, when they were hustled over in a very unbecoming manner.'

Much to the horror of everyone, including Lewis Morris (of the Morris brothers of Môn, and father of William Morris, who was a customs officer at Holyhead and Beaumaris), Judge Martyn remained in such a drunken state that he discharged all the prisoners, although they were obviously guilty. In a poem, which was to become a popular ballad, Lewis Morris passionately spoke out against their freedom, and protested for them to be hanged. The following verse gives us some idea of how strongly the people along the coast felt about the unholy deeds of the wreckers.

'How fine to the good and honest
Is the light of candle and fire;
How fine the brigands of the night
Is to be darkened houses;

How fine to my ears is it to hear
Of the hanging of the Thieves of Grigyll.

It is a village without the fear of God
Where evil lives in the hearts of men,
Bandits of the waves, vicious villains
Hiding their lanterns under their cloaks;
May God keep innocent travellers
From wrecking on the rocks of Grigyll.'

The coast of Ynys Môn has not been without its mysteries, too. The Pacific was a wooden paddle-steamer that had already made a name for herself in May 1851, when she set a new record for crossing the Alantic in nine days, twenty hours and ten minutes. In the January of 1856, however, the Pacific set a very different record. The two thousand nine hundred vessel left Liverpool for New York. It appears that the last piece of land she sighted was the coast of Anglesey before she disappeared – into thin air. Nothing was ever heard of her again. No messages were received, no wreckage was found, no corpses or any clues that she had ever existed. She quite simply vanished, as did the one hundred and eighty-six people on board.

Another ship that appeared, at first sight, to be another ghost ship was the Flower of Portsay, which had been en route from Kinsale to Garston with a cargo of timber. On the last day of August, 1908, a gale swept the Irish Sea. An alert from the lighthouse keepers along the Ynys Môn coast caused the Cemlyn lifeboat crew to launch their boat into the howling gale. A ship had been glimpsed drifting eastward, but she had since disappeared into the darkness. Both the Cemlyn and Bull Bay lifeboats searched through the night, but it was not found until morning. It had run aground in a narrow channel after crashing into the West Mouse rocks. The lifeboat men boarded her, found no sign of life and feared the worst. What had actually happened was that she had almost come to grief on the Skerries, losing both her anchors and sails. The order was given to abandon ship, and the crew of four lowered a boat and rowed to shore. This had not been easy with the howling wind and high seas, but they were lucky to be thrown onto the beach. The crew had managed to stagger to a local farm where they were given a hot meal and dry clothes. In the meantime the ship refloated herself, largely due to the cargo of timber, and began to drift on its aimless voyage until discovered by the lifeboatmen. They found some extra sails which they managed to rig, and towed the vessel back to Holyhead. As a reward for their gallant efforts, the lifeboat crew received a substantial amount of the salvage money.

In the 1820s the rector of Llanfair-yng-Nghornwy, the Reverend James Williams, was the first person in Wales to receive the RNLI Gold Medal. This was awarded for his bravery in riding on horseback to save five people from drowning. His wife, Frances Williams founded the Anglesey Association for the Preservation of Life from Shipwrecks. Together they raised funds to place lifeboats around the Ynys Môn coast, and it was through this initiative that the modern-day RNLI evolved. It is largely due to her efforts that the first lifeboat station in North Wales was established.

Frances Williams is one of Wales's great heroines, a lady of compassion, courage and enterprise, who is so often forgotten by the history books. As a girl growing up near the coast, she heard many dreadful accounts of disasters to shipping and wrecks, on the rock. On 26 March 1823, as a young married woman, she witnessed the wreck of the Irish sailing packet Alert which went aground on West Mouse. Strangely this was not because of high winds, but because it was becalmed on a fine, windless day. In full view of the shore, just a mile away, the packet drifted aimlessly in the pull of the strong tide, and ran aground unable to save herself. The tragedy was all the greater because the ship, being a packet boat, was crowded with people. She sank almost immediately and only seven people managed to reach safety, using one of the ship's boats. One hundred and forty-five lives were lost and only twenty-seven bodies were recovered.

The full impact of this tragedy haunted the young Frances because there was no boat available to go to the Alert's aid. If only, Frances had thought, some sort of life-saving boat could be provided, which would be on hand if a ship needed assistance. Such a boat could save lives which were, otherwise, lost unnecessarily when a vessel ran into difficulties. The enterprising Frances began to raise money. In 1821 she had been at Holyhead when King George IV landed there after his state visit to Ireland. She painted a picture of the scene and had this lithographed for sale from which she raised the substantial sum of nearly sixty pounds. She used the money to start a fund called the King's Landing Fund, which was to help save life at sea, and also encouraged future activities in this direction.

In March 1824 the Royal National Institution for the Preservation of Life from Shipwreck was founded. By 1850, about a hundred lifeboats were in service. Thirty of these belonged to the Institution, and the remainder provided by local societies such as that founded by Frances Williams and her husband.

On the foundation of the RNLI (as the Institution was to be re-named in 1854) Frances and her husband, together with their co-workers, immediately pledged their support. Frances urged her husband to write to the institution to tell of their own efforts. This resulted in a regular exchange of information and correspondence passing between the little Anglesey rectory, and the offices of the Institution.

In 1828, largely due to Frances' efforts, the first life-boat had been delivered and stationed at Cemlyn. Frances and her husband raised more funds for another boat which was to be built locally, and stationed at Holyhead. On 10 December of that year they organised a public meeting at Beaumaris at which the Anglesey Association for the Preservation of Life from Shipwreck was formed, and the Rev. James Williams appointed its first treasurer.

The waters around the Welsh coast were so dangerous that many masters of ships were reluctant to navigate some water-ways or harbours. Instead, they would ask for the assistance of a local pilot who knew the waters well. These men were a special breed who faced many dangers for others, often at risk to themselves.

An extremely interesting log book of one of these Ynys Môn pilots, Henry Edwards, Swellies Pilot, No 8, is kept at Anglesey County Library. He began his book with a flourish in January 1867, with the words:

'When I am dead and in my grave
And all my bones are rotten
Here's the book you'll see my name
When I am quite forgotten.'

The book covers a period of eleven years in which he noted the names of all the vessels he piloted through the Menai Straits, and the fees he received. Other interesting snippets of information such as the weather, pieces of verse, loans to friends, accidents, incidents, and even details of birth, deaths and marriages, were also recorded. One of the high-spots of his career is noted on 5 September 1879 when he piloted the Queen's Yacht Vice Versa into harbour.

CHAPTER TWENTY-ONE

THE LOSS OF THE ROYAL CHARTER AND OTHER WRECKS

Wrecks, as we have seen from the previous chapter are common-place around the Welsh coast. One of the most notable is the Royal Charter, which went aground in 1859, but before we learn about this wreck, perhaps we should look at a couple of other less famous disasters.

The first recorded collision in the waters off Holyhead took place on 20 February 1841, though there had been a number of such unrecorded disasters in the past. On this occasion the American sailing ship Governor Fencer, was en route from Liverpool to New York, carrying a cargo of iron, when she collided in thick fog with the paddle steamer Nottingham. The impact must have been horrific, for the bows of the Governor Fenner were smashed and she sunk almost immediately. There were one hundred and twenty-three on board, mostly emigrants on their way to make a new life in the United States, who all lost their lives. The paddle steamer, which was carrying cattle and sheep, seems to have faired better as it did manage to dock safely, although badly damaged. No record of what happened to the animals exists, so we are not certain whether they survived the tragedy.

Some forty years later, however, on the Irish sea route between Holyhead and Dublin, another tragic collision occurred, and the animal travellers were not so fortunate. This did not happen in fog but during the night – at midnight in fact, on October 31 1883. It involved the German sailing barge Alhambra and the London and North Western Railway's cattle steamship Holyhead. Both vessels were packed with cattle. As a result of the collision, both ships sank taking fifteen men, as well as all of the cattle.

As I have said, one of the best known wrecks off the Welsh coast, and one of the greatest peace-time disasters in British maritime history, must be the loss of the Royal Charter. The seven hundred and nineteen ton luxury steam clipper was bound for Liverpool from Australia, with four hundred and ninety-eight people on board, when she was struck by a hurricane and ran aground just a few miles from Moelfre.

The story of the Royal Charter began with the Australian Gold Rush and the need to build fast ships to carry men and bullion. At the time she was the fastest clipper, made of iron, and equipped with auxiliary steam power as well as sail. Once gold had been discovered in Australia people were emigrating in their droves to make their fortune. Between 1852 and 1857 over 200,000 people, including 4,000 Welshmen had landed on the Australian coast. These journeys were often horrific and frequently ships were becalmed, sometimes for weeks on end. The passengers were usually put on the lowest deck, even lower than the cattle, which meant that large numbers of people died on the journey. It has been recorded that up to one hundred deaths were common, hence the need for faster ships.

The Royal Charter was designed for speed and achieved a new record on her maiden voyage, such that her owners were able to boast that passengers could reach Australia in under sixty days. She was Welsh built, at the Sandycroft iron-works on the River Dee (Afon Ddyfrdwy) in Flintshire but was dogged with bad luck from the beginning. Because the Dee was so narrow at this point it was decided to launch her sideways but when they tried in 1855, she stayed put! A trench was dug to assist her to float, but even while the diggers were resting after their hard work, she went aground on a sandbank. Her main keel was bent, and she had to be taken to Liverpool for repair.

When the time eventually came for her maiden voyage, it was thought that the very tall masts may make her unstable. To alleviate this problem a large amount of stone ballast was put into the hold with the cargo on top, but because there was more cargo than first thought, the ship's main deck was now only six feet above the waterline. In this condition she set out from Liverpool to Australia on 18 January, 1856. The crew soon realised that the extra ballast was not necessary and was making her drag so that the propeller shaft almost broke. A week into her voyage, in a gale off Finisterre, the condition became so desperate that the Captain considered returning to England despite the effect that this would have on the ship, and the owner's reputation. As well as difficulties with the machinery, he was aware that water was slopping over the sides of the vessel, and that the lower decks were awash soaking everything, including the passengers in the third class and their belongings. Nothing could be done until the ballast was removed, and Captain Boyce therefore turned about and headed for Plymouth, steaming into Plymouth Sound on January 26. On February 16, minus the ballast, she set off once more, this time on her triumphant record-breaking run which was to take her to Melbourne in under sixty days.

By 1859, the Royal Charter had become a famous ship. She was luxurious and fast and a great asset to her owners. In August of that year she prepared to sail from Melbourne with more than just her usual quota of passengers and cargo aboard. From a small steamer the Royal Charter was loaded with small wooden boxes, carefully checked by the Captain and an Australian customs officer. Each box was marked with its weight, the name of the shipper, and the bank for which it was consigned and carefully stored in the strong room, deep within the hull. These containers were full of the treasure that had encouraged so many to emigrate to Australia – gold, then valued at four pounds sterling per ounce. As we can imagine, the cargo was heavily guarded on its way to the ship and after loading, the Captain handed over a receipt for the staggering sum of £322,440. In fact there was more gold than the Captain's receipt guaranteed, for many of the passengers were carrying their own personal fortunes with them in money-belts or amongst their luggage. James Dean, a smith who had gone out from England to make his fortune, had been lucky and was carrying a cheque for a considerable amount of money safely tucked away in a waterproof belt.

On August 26 1859 the Royal Charter sailed out of Melbourne with approximately three hundred and ninety passengers on board. Her Captain was Thomas Taylor, who had been a passenger on her maiden voyage and who, by all accounts, was a rough diamond who had risen from the ranks on his own merit, and was considered an excellent commander and seaman. He was strict and proud, but he had reason to be – he was the commander of the famous Royal Charter, and he ran her well.

The vessel had completed two months of her journey, sailing non-stop round Cape Horn and sighting the southern coast of Ireland on 24 October. Here she stopped to allow passengers ashore at Queenstown and many of those remaining on board wrote letters to be posted ashore, letters which were to become tragic and touching memories for their friends and relatives. That evening, the passengers, in high spirits, presented a testimonial to Captain Taylor to show their appreciation for the ship and the excellent voyage so far. In return he promised that he would get them to Liverpool within twenty four hours.

During the morning of the following day the weather began to worsen and the sails were taken in off the coast of Caernarfonshire. At 1.30 p.m the Royal Charter passed Holyhead island in calm seas, although hazy fog lay inland. But there was nothing to hint that anything out of the ordinary was about to happen. At 4.30 p.m., the vessel passed the harbour at Holyhead amid much excitement, past the monster steamship, Great Eastern, as it lurked in the breakwater, too large to enter the harbour. Soon after, hurricane winds broke. Captain Taylor had the choice of sheltering at Holyhead or attempting to make it to Liverpool. He decided to continue, rather than delay the voyage, as he had to maintain the reputation of making the journey from Melbourne to Liverpool 'in under 60 days'. Also he had promised his passengers that they would reach Liverpool within twenty four hours of leaving Queenstown, and he was not a man to break his word.

With seventy miles to go there was nothing to warn him that the hurricane was gathering speed. However, by 6 o'clock in the evening, when the ship had rounded the Skerries, the storm changed, and the strength of the wind increased. Still there were no real warning signs, but the winds kept turning in a circle. As a result the Royal Charter found herself being driven onto the Anglesey shore, with no room to manoevre and nowhere to run. At 6.30 she sent off rockets and fired guns as a signal for a pilot, and showed a blue light to ask for assistance. The signals were seen by two Liverpool pilot boats and also by a member of Pilot Boat No 11, but the weather had become so bad that, even if they had been able to reach her, they could never have been able to board her.

Aboard the Royal Charter the Captain's efforts to control her were failing and about 10 p.m. it was evident that she was drifting towards the shore, a situation fraught with disaster, so the Captain gave the order: 'Prepare to let go anchors.' He tried in vain to turn the ship so that she could run into the Irish sea, rather than on to the rocky coast of Anglesey. When this failed, at 11p.m. he give the order for the port anchor to be released. The Royal Charter seemed steadier and the Captain, crew and passengers relaxed, although they knew they were still in a desperate situation.

As the Captain was reassuring passengers, especially the women who were still up and ordering coffee, the port cable broke and he returned to the deck to cope with this desperate situation. At about 2.30am the final disaster struck when the starboard anchor cable parted and the ship drove straight into the land that was invisible in the darkness. Distress guns exploded into the night and rockets lit up the sky but no help came. Around 3 am, in sheer desperation to try and save his ship, the Captain ordered the masts to be cut away. The passengers were roused, and for the first time told of the danger. Their terror and panic did not help the situation, especially as the ship had been struck. Tremors shook the ship beneath the passengers feet but she had not been holed. The Captain sent an apprentice boy down to reassure those crowded below decks that everything was fine. But the boy's words went unheeded. According to Edward Wilson, an Able Seaman, who later described what happened:

'There was nothing but confusion on deck, fore and aft passengers, saloon, cabin and steerage all mixed together, fathers and mothers clasping their children in their arms, wives clinging to their husbands, shrieking, and crying.'

Eventually the Captain himself appeared looking cool and in control. 'Now ladies,' he declared,' you need not be at all afraid. We are on a sandy beach, and embedded in the sand. We are not ten paces from the shore, and the tide will leave us dry, and in ten minutes you will all be safe.' His calming voice had the desired effect, and the passengers began to prepare to go ashore. What the Captain did not know was that the ship was indeed aground, but had been driven sideways on by the waves; the tide, now on the turn, was not about to let go. Waves pounded the ship and tossed foaming waters onto the passengers making it difficult for them to keep their footing. When finally dawn broke the Captain, crew and passengers could not believe their eyes. They were aground a mere twenty-five yards (twenty-three metres) from land! This short distance was all that separated them from the rocks and headland. However, between the ship and the rocks, the sixty foot (eighteen metre) high waves thundered in a terrifying manner, such that it seemed impossible to bridge the gap between them. The decision was taken to rig up a boson's chair so that those on board could reach safety. A Maltese seaman, Joseph Rodgers, volunteered to swim ashore where he was dragged, exhausted and cold, to safety by the rapidly increasing crowd of villagers, and taken to a nearby cottage to recover. Frantic attempts were made to rig up a boson's chair after which the passengers were able to reach safety, battered and drenched by the huge waves.

The breakers continued to pound the vessel and drive her further inland until, around 7 a.m., the ship gave a lurch and hit the stony ledges and rocks, which were not visible from above. She snapped in two, and enormous waves washed through her from stem to stern, taking the remaining screaming passengers with them. Many were crushed between the two halves of the ship, battered by the waves, thrown ashore, or too shocked by what had happened to move. Horribly mutilated bodies mingled with the living, as torn off limbs, and even heads were dashed by the sea. The scenes were ghastly and made more terrible because, after sailing safely halfway across the world, the great vessel was destroyed only a couple of yards from land, with many of her passengers dying in full view of those who had gathered, powerless to help after the alarm had been raised by a Moelfre man. During the terrible storm in the night, part of his roof had been ripped off by the wind. As soon as it became light, he went up to see what he could do. He looked out to sea and was the first to know of the wreck of the Royal Charter. He raised the alarm.

All tragedies have their sad tales to recall. One young seaman, Isaac Lewis, who was a Moelfre man, whilst waiting to sit in the boson's chair recognized his father among the crowds of rescuers on shore. Desperately he is said to have cried out, 'Oh father, I have come home to die.' No one is quite sure what happened, but he was either swept from the boson's chair by a huge wave, or managed to reach safety and was dragged back by the waves. However, he did not survive and his body was washed ashore less than a mile from his home.

Of the up to four hundred and ninety-eight people on board no accurate numbers exist. It is thought that only thirty-eight survived, and none were women or children. Most strange was the fact that very few actually met their death by drowning, and no survivors could say exactly what happened or why it happened, except that within the space of a few moments, the Royal Charter was doomed.

The whole country was shocked by the disaster, and for a while Ynys Môn was invaded by reporters who were after a sensational story. Among them was a young author, Charles Dickens. He came around Christmas time, lodged at Amlwch, and went to Moelfre everyday to investigate and record the event. He wrote a dramatic account in The Uncommercial Traveller. When he returned, two months later, he reported that the stains and outlines where the bodies had lain could still be seen on the church floor.

The four hundred and sixty people who lost their lives were laid out in the small church of Llanallgo or in the villagers cottages, to await identification. Soon relatives and mourners hurried from all parts of the world to this remote little spot of Wales. Many found the scenes unbearable, and the rector and his wife helped out by asking relatives for details, and making the initial search themselves in an attempt to lessen the stress. When they found the correct body they took the mourners blindfolded, and only removed the blindfold for identification to be made. Most of the victims were buried in local churchyards, although the villagers, whilst sympathetic, feared there would be no place left for them when their time came.

The rector of Llanallgo, the Rev Stephen Roose Hughes, was a gentle man who in an indirect way became a victim of the Royal Charter himself. It is claimed that he wrote over a thousand letters to relatives and friends of the victims and that the strain of the long days and nights spent with the dead and comforting the bereaved proved too much for him. He died only two years later at the age of forty-seven.

Three hundred thousand pounds worth of gold was recovered but the remainder was unaccounted for. Several attempts have been made to recover the balance, but with little success. Divers worked under the most appalling conditions but only a very small quantity of gold-dust and three hundred sovereigns have been recovered. Rumours spread that some locals were, by studying the tides, able to determine where to look amongst the rocks for the spoils, and reaped the rich harvest. There may be some truth in this story as, not so many years ago, when on old cottage near Moelfre was being modernised, a bag of gold thought to have come from the wreck, was found lodged in the chimney.

All that remains today of that terrible day is the wreck itself, which still lies off the Anglesey coast in eighteen feet (five metres) of water. At Llanallgo churchyard there is an obelisk in memory of those who lost their lives, and a plaque on it gives a brief account of what happened. Any visitor to the area will feel sad as they try to conjure up the gruesome scenes that must have confronted the people of Llanallgo all those years ago and, as you walk quietly by, perhaps you would like to hope and pray that the victims are now at rest.

By some odd coincidence, exactly one hundred years after the wreck of the Royal Charter, a more modern vessel was also wrecked in a hurricane, in the very same bay. On 27 October, 1959, only the day after a special service had been held at Llanallgo Church to commemorate the sinking of the Royal Charter, the six hundred and fifty ton steamer Hindlea, came to a sad end.

The coxswain of the Moelfre lifeboat, Richard Evans, received a telephone call that a coaster sheltering in Dulas Bay had started to drag her anchor. He quickly gathered together a skeleton crew of four, of whom one, Hugh Jones, had never been out on a rescue before, and put out in a reserve boat, the Edmund & Mary Robinson, as the official Moelfre lifeboat was being refitted. In twenty-five feet waves and one hundred miles an hour winds, the lifeboat crew found the Hindlea holding by one cable. Even though she was heading for sure destruction, her captain would not give the order to abandon ship for another half hour, when she was just two hundred yards from the rocks. As the lifeboat moved towards the Hindlea, the lifeboat was thrown onto its beam end but managed to right herself. Coxwain Richard Evans tried for a second time to approach the doomed ship but this time the lifeboat was hurled into the side of the Hindlea. Richard Evans tried no less than eight more times to approach the Hindlea, and each time another crew member of the Hindlea jumped to safety. Despite the raging gale no lives were lost, and within a short time of the rescue the Hindlea was thrown against the rocks and shattered – just half a mile or so from the wreck of the Royal Charter.

For his valiant efforts Richard Evans was awarded the RNLI Gold Medal and in 1966 went on to win a second one when he rescued ten men from the Greek freighter Nafsoporos, when she encountered a severe gale off the West Mouse.

The other notable wreck in the area was that of Rothsay Castle on Dutchman's Bank when one hundred lives were lost. On 17 August 1831, at 11 o'clock in the morning the steam packet set sail from Liverpool bound for Beaumaris. Most of the passengers were holiday-makers and registered in the books, but a large number joined the ship at the pier-head. It is quite possible that the boat was over-crowded and it has been estimated that at least one hundred and thirty passengers were on board, in addition to the crew and a band.

Soon after leaving Liverpool, a strong wind sprang-up, and when the ship was about fifteen miles from shore, many of the passengers became alarmed at the rough sea. The ship was due to reach Beaumaris by seven in the evening, but when darkness fell it was still far from it's destination. Just before mid-night it entered the Menai Straits – about five or six miles from Beaumaris. It appears that the vessel had been letting in water throughout the journey and near Ynys Seiriol, water flowed over the coals and the engines failed. The vessel was caught by a strong gale and driven onto the dreaded 'Dutchman's Bank where it became stuck in the sand.

The captain is said to have remained unperturbed and refused to fire a gun or use a distress signal. Some of the passengers sounded the alarm bell, ringing it with such violence that the clapper broke and continued to strike it with a stone or piece of coal. The bell was heard at Beaumaris but, as no lights had been hoisted at the mast of the steamer, the searchers were unable to find the vessel even though the moon was reported to be shining in a clear sky! Interestingly, shortly afterwards, the captain of the vessel stumbled overboard and was the first person drowned. He was quickly followed by his mate.

Great waves were now breaking over the ship. A boat was launched, and the passengers crowded onto it but it was impossible for it to float in such a sea. The storm increased. One survivor related how, in the pale moonlight, he saw the passengers huddled together, praying and crying as waves broke over both sides of the vessel. The steward and his wife lashed themselves to the mast, having resolved to live or die together. Their bodies were later found locked in each other's arms. Parents sought to protect their children and one mother with her baby in her arms, was swept away by a enormous wave. In the seething sea, she held her baby aloft but before long both disappeared from sight.

It has been recorded that John Nuttal of Bury and five others clambered onto a portion of wreckage only two-and-a-half yards square. Among them was the son of the helmsman, who was saved from being washed into the heavy seas by climbing onto Mr Nuttal's back and clinging tight around his neck. The courageous Mr Nuttal further risked his own life by reaching over the side of the flimsy 'raft' to grasp hold of a young woman by her hair as she swept past them. Two other people were picked up and, after being tossed about for hours, all nine were rescued.

Another person who was rescued was Mr Rutland who played in the band. He was swept overboard but had the presence of mind to take with him his bass drum and clinged to it for hours.

Harriet Martineau told a story of two men who clung to the same piece of wood that was not big enough for both. One wanted to let go because he was old, the other because he was young and felt he could swim to safety. They both let go at the same moment but managed to reach the shore and come face to face with each other again.

These are just a few of the interesting stories of some of the twenty two passengers who were saved from the wreck of the Rothsay Castle. In 1832 an ode about the loss of the Rothsay Castle was written for the Eisteddfod held at Beaumaris Castle, the year following the incident. Also Princess Victoria, who was attending with her mother, the then Duchess of Kent, was presented with a set of drawings of 'artist's impressions' of the tragic loss of Rothsay Castle, all bound in gold trimmed morocco.

CHAPTER TWENTY-TWO

ANGLESEY FOLKLORE, TRADITIONS AND CUSTOMS

Ynys Môn, like every other area in Wales, has its own set of traditions and customs. Some we have already encountered, but there are others that I am sure will fascinate the reader, and allow a glimpse into a time when tradition was more important to the community than it is in our enlightened age.

Many people who do not know the island may think of it as some remote and isolated place, beyond the reach of influences from other parts. But you will be surprised to learn that in the 18th century, even English folk tunes were widely known on the island. Lewis and Richard Morris, whom we met in chapter eighteen, made a substantial contribution to our knowledge of the folk culture of Ynys Môn by leaving an extensive list of Môn customs from that period. Richard Morris contributed by recording a list of tunes in 1717, which have included numerous wassail-songs belonging to the celebration of Candlemass (February 2). This is the Feast of the Purification of the Virgin Mary, known as Gwyl Fair y Canhwyllau (Mary's Festival of Candles).

The lengthening of days which followed the Christmas festivities brought a promise of spring, new hope, and re-birth of plant life to the countryman. During this change from winter to spring, the feast of Candlemas held an important place in the lives of the people who, like the inhabitants of Môn, relied so much on the land for their existence. Candlemas was seen as a time when artificial light could be dispensed with, and the animals could be fed before dark. The feast derives from the pre-Reformation ceremony of blessing the candles and distributing them amongst the people, who afterwards carried them in a solemn procession This was a time when parties of carollers wandered through the Môn countryside in search of good cheer, warmth and a friendly hearth. The custom, which included a competition of verse at the door, was followed by a sober procession into the kitchen. A second carol was sung, followed by a request for a chair to be placed in the middle of the floor. A young girl with a child, representing Mary and her Child, would be found to represent the Holy pair. After singing y Garol Gadair (the chair carol) the party then filed in slow procession around the chair and its occupants. Another carol was asked for, then the wassailing bowl, a vessel filled with a drink (usually of mulled wine or ale), was served by the man of the house. The young girl would then be offered the bowl and asked to drink, and to give some to the child, before passing it on to the carollers. The girl then would rise from the chair and move away as another carol was being sung.

Another custom recorded by Lewis Morris, and which survives today, is the clapping for Easter Eggs. This takes place the Monday before Easter, and is known on the island as Clepain wyau. Some of the wooden clappers used can be seen at the Welsh Folk Museum at St Fagans. The Môn children, whilst begging for eggs would chant the words: 'Clap, clap, gofyn wy i hogiau bach ar y plwy' (Clap, clap, ask for an egg for little boys on the parish). After the chant, the noise of the clappers would be enough to indicate the nature of the request. It is said that, in the Amlwch area, children would collect as many as forty eggs in this way. Sometimes they were given pennies instead of eggs, but in certain homes they would be turned away with the chant, 'The cat hasn't laid any yet!' From the earliest times the egg has been the symbol of fertility and the re-generation of life, and at Easter time hard-boiled eggs were dyed and rolled about the grass until they were broken, before being eaten.

Our ancestors also observed a period of fasting during Lent, the forty days preceding Easter, to commemorate Christ's abstinence from temptation. Lent commences on Ash Wednesday and it was the day preceding the beginning of Lent that was important to our ancestors. It was natural to use up all the forbidden foods before the fasting. In England we find reference to Collop Monday, the day before Shrove Tuesday when the last meat dish was eaten. Welsh records do not record this custom, but they do illustrate the practice of eating the last supplies of fat, butter and eggs in the form of pancakes on Shrove Tuesday. Blawta a blonega, or the collecting of flour and fats on Shrove Tuesday to make pancakes was usually carried out by the poor and the children of the district. However some verses show that pancakes, rather than the ingredients, were asked for:

Please may I have a pancake
My mouth is watering for a pancake
My mother is too poor to buy the flour
And my father is too lazy to work.

Records show that, during the early part of this century, Môn children were often seen returning home with their faces covered, from ear to ear, with treacle and fat, and no doubt a stomach ache too!

May Day also brought its own set of unique customs. On Môn the eve of May Day was important for young men who had lost their sweethearts to another man. It was the custom for the youth to make a straw effigy of the successful lover, and to place it near the window of the unfaithful girl, or in a prominent place near her home. Onto the effigy he would pin a letter. This usually ended in a fight, which would take place at the May fair. May Day began with the singing of May carols, and everyone generally having a good time.

An interesting custom of North Wales which was kept alive until 1890, particularly in Caernarfonshire and Môn, was the traditional wedding with the race from the church door to the house where the wedding feast was to take place. It began immediately the ring was placed on the brides finger and the reward for the fastest runner would be a piece of the wedding cake. In Môn, like many other parts of Wales, the wedding began with the bridal party and the guests marching to church, if horses could not be afforded. Lewis Morris in his writings referred to bridal parties on their way to church enjoying themselves by dancing, accompanied by a fiddler or harpist.

The gathering of the harvest was the last major agricultural task of the year and, on an agreed date, both men and women helped in the cutting and binding of the wheat. The day would end with a special harvest supper which included a dish, called whipod, which consisted of rice, white bread, raisins, currants, treacle and other ingredients, This would be followed by dancing and games.

There are many stories connected with All-Hallows Eve, concerning marriage. For example, in Môn it is said that

'three shell snails from the church wall, be put under a leaf on a table, will write the name of sweetheart.

Ghosts, it appears, are as common on the island as anywhere else, and there is a belief that if a person saw a ghost he would soon die. However, there are also tales of ghosts of living people appearing before others. One concerns the mate of an Anglesey ship travelling westwards who told the captain that there was a stranger in the cabin, writing. The captain went to investigate and found no one there, but on a piece of paper was a message requesting the captain to change course. After much debate he decided to accede to the request and they soon came across a vessel sinking. On board were three hundred people, and all were saved. When the mate met the captain of the sinking ship, he swore that the skipper was the stranger he had seen writing in the cabin.

Another tale concerns a farm house call Clwchdernog in the parish of

Llanddeusant, which was said to have been haunted by a spirit. It appears that no one was prepared to speak to the ghost, although it was seen by several people. One evening during the mid 1880's, John Hughes of Bodedern visited the house. He was a widower, and had come to see one of the servant girls there in the hope of finding a second Mrs Hughes. The ghost appeared in the room with John and the girl. John was, obviously, frightened but decided to speak to the ghost, and asked him why he troubled the house.

'Have I wronged you in any way?' John asked the ghost.

'No,' came the reply.

John then pointed to the girl and asked if she was the cause of the ghostly visits.

'No,' came the reply again.

John then went through the names of all the people living in the house asking if any of these disturbed the ghost. On each occasion the reply was no.

Frustrated with the replies John then asked if no one in the house disturbed the ghost, why did he continue to disturb the occupiers.

The ghost replied, ' There are treasures hidden on the south side of Ffynnon Wen which belong, and must be given, to the nine month old baby in this house. When this is done, I will never disturb the household again.' Hughes promised to go to the place and the following day started to dig. Soon he came upon an iron chest filled with gold, silver and other valuable items. John collected up the contents and took them to the child's parents, explained about the ghost, and told them to keep the items until the child came of an age to take possession of them himself. The ghost was never seen in the house again.

The ceremony that follows the death of a person was usually the preparation of the corpse for burial. The death was formally announced by the parish-bell, and the house where the corpse lay was called ty corff (the corpse house). The corpse would be washed and prepared for the coffin. Meanwhile the carpenter would have called at the house and measured the body before making the coffin. When the body had been placed in the coffin, measures were taken to prevent decay. In some areas it was a pewter plate with a quantity of salt on it. Other districts used bread or paper. On the night before the funeral the gwylnos (vigil) was kept. The day after the gwylnos, all who had been present would visit the ty corff again, to take part in the funeral. In Môn during the 18th century, the mourners would be given a cup of drink and, if the deceased was rich, cake and wine would be served. Sometimes, after the guests had formed the funeral procession wine and finger biscuits were handed around. In

Môn when the drink, which was a jug of mulled ale and lemon peel, appeared the men took off their hats and, in silence, presented the jug to each guest in turn, who took a sip and handed it back to the attendant.

Llanfechell is a scattered parish, but the most interesting feature is the odd shaped tower of the 12th century church. It was built by a local squire who, according to tradition, objected to the sound of the bells because their vibration spoiled the beer he brewed.

CHAPTER TWENTY-THREE

LITTLE KNOWN RESORTS AND BAYS

Anglesey has many resorts and bays which can be easily missed. Some have an interesting history, an unusual story to relate, or an interesting theory concerning its name. Others are worth a visit purely for their beauty, wildlife or flora, but visitors should always be aware of the nesting birds. As with other chapters this could turn into a book of its own and therefore,I have selected those I consider most worthy of a visit.

First we shall visit Porth Llechog (Bull Bay) which is situated three kilometres north-west of Amlwch on the A5025. It takes its name from a neighbouring inlet in the rock bound coast. It was originally called Porth Llechog by a Welshman who, having sailed from Nefyn, was driven by a northerly gale into the shelter of the bay. He was just about to give up hope of ever being found alive when he noticed the little cove behind Trwyn Melyn. Afterwards he settled down in the district and named the cove, as well as his house, Llechog, which loosely means 'excellent shelter' Although Bull Bay now relies on tourism, in the early years of the 19th century it played its part in the local shipbuilding boom, and was also a thriving fishing port. From here a dozen or so fishermen would set sail for the fishing grounds four miles out to sea where they would catch cod to sell at a shilling apiece.

An interesting feature of the bay is a swimming pool, which was built in 1864 by Mr Evan Pritchard for the Marquess of Anglesey. The pool measures twenty yards by ten, is shaped out of solid rock, and is replenished with fresh sea water by each tide. The entrance is lined by a medieval style gateway with round towers, containing guard rooms. Inside is a small walled court lined with stone dressing rooms and ornamental flowerbeds, from which a sloping subterranean pathway leads into the pool.

A lifeboat station was established here between 1868 and 1926, during which time the lifeboat was required on forty occasions, and saved a total of sixty-three lives.

Trwyn Eilian (Point Lynas) was once an old Pilot Station. The original name for Point Lynas was Trwyn Balog (which can be rather rudely translated as the Jutting Point), but since the 18th century it has, maybe thankfully, also been known as Point Lynas, a corrupt form of Eleanus, so named after Saint Eilian whose church and well are situated across the waters of Porth Eilian. The Pilot Station was established in 1781, when a white pilot house was erected on the headland together with a flagstaff for day signals, and two small reflecting lamps placed in the upper windows at night. The first known keeper was Robert Beavor, the son of an Aberffraw schoolmaster, who was also a Captain of Privateers during the America War of Independence. We know that he was stationed here in 1797 but it appears he had done the job for a while before that. The minutes of the meetings of the pilot's committee in August 1797 reads:

'Mr Robert Beavor the Governor of the Lighthouse at Point Lynas his Petition to this Committee prays for some allowance to be paid to him annually for such services as he has for many years done for the Pilots without any payment for the same. This Committee assembled were of opinion that from this office he ought to be allowed and paid Twenty Five Pounds a year, by quarterly payments. This Committee also recommended that an order be made that each Pilot Boat at proper seasons of the year do as formally they did carry coals in bags for Mr Beavor's use at the Point of Lynas and deliver them safe there.'

Mr Beavor died in 1814 at the age of 65, and his grave can be seen in Llaneilian churchyard across the water.

St Eilian came to the area in the 6th century with his family, supposedly bringing with them cattle in a ship from Rome. They landed at Porthyrychain, near Amlwch, and if the visitor is extremely observant he or she will be able to see the marks of oxen hooves embedded in the rocks. At the time, Caswallon Lawhir was the prince of Gwynedd and lord of the land. Tradition relates that, owing to some crime against the church, St Eilian excommunicated the prince and caused him to be struck blind as a penance. It was only thanks to the prayers of the saint, that his sight was restored. As a thank you, Caswallon promised St Eilian that he would give him whatever land he wanted to found a church. St Eilian had a young male deer, so he apparently told Caswallon that he would take as much land and ground as his hart could gain in running from all your greyhounds. The chase began from Bryn Dulas and was bounded by Mynydd Parys, Amlwch and Porth Eilian. All the land, men, wood, waters and fields within this boundary were given to the saint.

Traeth Coch (Red Wharf Bay) is the Mecca for botanists and the rock pools along the shore are extremely interesting and display a fine collection of anemones and other marine creatures. The large limestone block, called Castell Mawr (resembles a ruined castle, and is situated at the mouth of the Afon Ceint (or Afon Nodwydd at this point). It is the site of an early Brython fortress, and was probably occupied during the Roman period as coins have been found there.

At the head of Traeth Coch is Pentraeth, which was once known as Llanfair Betws Geraint; it is the chapelry of Llanddyfnan and is dedicated to the Virgin Mary, but was founded by St Geraint, a 5th century saint. However, one legend relates that St Geraint was the grandson of Cystennin, king of Dumnonia (in Cornwall), who might have been a successor of King Arthur and grandfather of Saint Aidan and St Cybi, and also an admiral who defended the coast of Wales against the Saxon army. Interestingly, about half a mile out of Pentraeth on the road to Beaumaris, is the entrance to Plas Gwyn, which is a country mansion. In a field nearby the visitor will see three stones in a line, said to be the site of a traditional contest. It appears that a man called Einion had a daughter whom Hywel Gwynedd, son of Owain Gwynedd, fancied. But Hywel had a rival, and it was agreed that the better of the two at leaping should win the girl as his bride. At a spot called Abernodwydd, Hywel won his prize over three leaps, and the three stones were erected to mark the extent of each leap. As for the rival, tradition tells us that he died on the spot of a broken heart.

Stretching almost from Beaumaris to the entrance of the Menai Straits sits a huge sandbank called Traeth Lafan, which is derived from wylofain, or the place of the weeping. Legend states that this area once housed a village which was overwhelmed by the sea, and that during the 19th century, entire oak trees were discovered at low tide in a region far from the present shoreline. To confirm this, in a churchyard in Abergele, on the mainland some way to the east, is the tomb of a man who lived in an area that lay three miles north of the sands, which is a very well submerged area today.

Before the Industrial Revolution, Cemaes was the main port on the north coast of the island, and a centre of shipbuilding, as well as a home to the smugglers. In the medieval period it was one of the administrative units of the island, a cantref (or a hundred). It has remained an attractive village with its little harbour, and a breakwater that shields the fishing and pleasure boats at their moorings. There is a sad legend attached to one of the caves in the Bay. It appears that many years ago, a young man lived near the Bay and had a violent row with his family. In a temper he mounted his dapple blue-grey horse and galloped furiously away from the house. He was in such a rage that he rode his horse right over the cliff-edge. His body was never found but the carcass of a horse was discovered washed into a cave, which became known as Ogof y March Glas (the cave of the blue horse). Perched high on the cliffs above the bay is Llanbadrig Church, one of only two Welsh churches dedicated to St Patrick. Legend has it that, during the 5th century, St Patrick was shipwrecked on an island which can be seen just off the coast. He made his way to the rocks below the present church, and found a cave, and then founded the church to thank God for his safety.

Trearddur was once called Tywyn-y-capel, but the name was changed at the beginning of the tourism heyday by a local landowner to distinguish it from such places as Tywyn near Aberdyfi, which had a similar name. He chose Trearddur, mailing it up from Tre-Iarddur – homestead of Iarddur, after the Welsh family of that name who were descended from Rhodri Fawr. On the main beach once stood the chapel of St Ffraid, who is the patron Saint of Trearddur. She was probably a contemporary of Saint Cybi, who is said to have arrived from Ireland floating on a piece of grass covered soil.

Legend tells us that she was born in the village of Fochart, in the diocese of Armagh in Ireland, and died around 523. She was known as the virgin of Kildare, and had a reputation for performing miracles. It is claimed that when she became a nun, her step-mother's leg was cut off, but on Ffraid's request another leg and foot grew in its place. It is also claimed that she extracted honey from a stone to give to a poor man who was hungry, and that when butter turned to ashes she took the ashes in her hand and turned them back into butter. It is also said that, when her father offered her in marriage to an Irish lord whom she did not love, she caused her own eyes to drop out and then when she was sure that the lord would not accept her, picked them up, washed them, and re-placed them. To prevent her father from finding her another suitor, she went with her maids to the Irish coast and, with a knife, cut a piece of green turf for each of them, Then, like ships, these pieces of turf carried them over the water to Ynys Môn, where she landed at Trearddur and built her chapel.

A little to the south of Trearddur is Towyn Lodge, a Georgian House which was occupied by Thomas Telford at the beginning of the 19th century whilst he was building the Menai Bridge. His workroom was a small tower in the corner of the garden, overlooking Bay.

On the south western side of Trearddur Bay is Ogof Betsi, a large cave. Nearby lived Dic Bach and his wife Betsi Fawr whose son had run away to sea. Whenever wreckage was swept ashore Dic and Betsi would go hunting for the spoils which they hid in the cave, safely out of reach of the tide. Betsi, as her full name suggests, was a large lady, and needed both her hands for clambering up the rock, so she would don an enormous pair of blue woollen breeches which would hold the goods as they came to hand – much to the amusement of the villagers.

One winter's evening a ship was wrecked and for days afterwards the tide brought in the spoils which, as was customary, the locals helped themselves to before the customs officials arrived to begin their salvage work. Several cases of whisky had been washed ashore and already a number of the villagers were in a state of stupor on the beach. While Dic went around pouring salt water into their mouths, 'to put out the flames of drink,' Betsi was busy opening a fresh case that she had found, and was storing the bottles in her breeches – six on each side. By now news had reached them that the custom officials had arrived. Betsi immediately thought of the cave, and decided it was time to disappear with her spoils. But for all the care with which she waddled up the beach, there was no mistaking the clink of the bottles.

'What have you got there?' shouted the custom man.

'Nothing' shouted Betsi, ' you can search me if you like.'

The official, realizing the delicacy of the matter, decided to give Betsi the benefit of the doubt, and she staggered away.

Minutes later Dic followed, none too sober, and much to his horror found Betsi among the slippery boulders, her face as white as death, and the air heavy with the smell of liquor. Further into the cave he found the lifeless body of their own son, where the tide had flung him – his first and final homecoming.

Rhosneigr is a rambling Edwardian seaside resort sitting four miles from the road, but is equally as attractive to the modern visitors, especially the windsurfers who flock to the Bay. At nearby Rhoscolyn the visitor can see the memorial to Tyger, mentioned in an earlier chapter. The area is famous for it marble which has been used in the building of Bristol, Peterborough and Worcester Cathedrals. In the 19th century, it was home to the oyster catching industry and had a china clay works. Today a workshop produces designer knitwear.

The cornerstone of the northern coast is Trwyn y Gader (Carmel Head) which is approached by narrow lanes. The head is fringed with dangerous rocks, and two navigation beacons stand on the north side with a third on the offshore island of Maen y Bugail (West Mouse). The area contains some of the finest Ynys Môn landscape.

Another excellent place to visit is Ogofau Ffyddlyn (caves) on the south west side of Trwyn y Gader. Winding down from the moors you will see a narrow ravine which leads down to the inlet, where once a small lake lay. Today the lake is silted and choked with reeds, but down this valley ran the telegraph poles and wires that established communication with the Skerries. However, long before this, Ffyddlyn cove was the landing place of the Viking rovers. It is claimed that one chieftain of a band of sea rovers, having overwhelmed the Welshmen, captured the daughter of a local chief, a beautiful damsel named Rhona, who he wanted for himself. She, on the other hand, was in love with the son of a neighbouring chief, and refused his advances. In his anger, the Viking ordered that the damsel be bound and carried to the great caves of Ffyddlyn where she would be left to drown if she would not agree to become his wife. Later, when he returned with several of his followers to hear her last words before the tide reached her, he was angered to see a young man cutting her bonds. The rover jumped forward and, with his sword raised, was about to slay the young man when a large rock fell from the top of the cave and became wedged between the walls. The other rovers were so horrified at the sudden death of their leader that they were unable to move, and the lovers took the opportunity to escape, although they fell on the slippery rocks on more than one occasion. At last they managed to reach the shore of Ffyddlyn and scrambled onto the island, where the young man had hidden his coracle. The young woman was exhausted and asked if they could rest for a minute or two, but by the time she had recovered the Vikings had reached the top of the island. Again, fate was on their side and the earth shook like the sound of thunder, and the island split across and a wide gulf lay between the couple and their pursuers. They made their escape and, as a reminder of the story, visitors today can see the chasm that spilts the island and the great rock wedged in the narrow throat of the cave.

CHAPTER TWENTY-FOUR

MODERN ANGLESEY

Today the tourist trade, plays as important a role as agriculture in keeping Ynys Môn alive. However, tourism also has the drawback of being very much a seasonal industry, and there is a need for the island to find new modern enterprises if it is to grow and evolve. Yet, despite these modern schemes and industries, the island conjures up to the onlooker the very essence of Wales – a land of inspiration.

We must never forget that Ynys Môn is a paradise for wildlife, and those who are interested in exploring the natural history should find a copy of 'A New Natural History of Anglesey', edited by W Eifion Jones and published by the Anglesey Antiquarian Society, Llangefni in 1990.

The area and its wildlife has inspired many people, like Charles F Tunnicliffe, a member of the Royal Academy, and one of Britain's most respected wildlife artists. He was so excited by the landscape, the people and bird-life that he made Malltraeth Bay his home from 1947 until he died in 1979. He was once asked why he came to London so infrequently. His reply was swift and succinct: 'I prefer the birds of Anglesey to those of Piccadilly'. A large collection of his watercolours and sketches were acquired at auction in 1981 by the island's administrators. A large part of the cost of four hundred thousand pounds was paid out of compensation from the oil companies for damage to the environment around the port of Amlwch. Some of these paintings can be seen at Oriel Ynys Môn, a centre in Llangefni where the visitor can enjoy the story of Angelsey, and experience the spirit of the island from the prehistoric age to the present.

Ynys Môn is an important breeding area for puffins, guillemots, razorbills, terns, cormorants and gulls. At South Stack the visitor may catch a glimpse of the rare chough, a member of the crow family. It is estimated that there are only one hundred breeding pairs in Wales, and usually six or more pairs nest here. There is also an abundance of flowers on South Stack, including rare species such as the spotted searose and pale heath violet. Most interesting of all is the South Stack fleawort, growing in its only known location in the world!

Inland at Llyn Alaw is the bird sanctuary, where a purpose built 'hide' will provide plenty of cover to enjoy views of wildlife and wader flocks. It is the primary water reservoir for the island and was created in 1966. When the water level is at its lowest, a large number of waders can be spotted on the lake bed.

For the more energetic, a guided coastal walk from the Anglesey

Coastal Heritage Centre, Llys Llywelyn Centre at Aberffraw, is essential. The centre has a natural environment and historical display, with an audio-visual theatre as well as an excellent craft centre. Not to be missed is the breath-taking pleasure of watching the sunset as it sets over Ynys Llanddwyn. It is truly one of life's unforgettable experiences. Whist in the area the visitor should make for Newborough Warren, where such interesting plants as dune pansies, sea surge and a variety of orchids, including marsh orchids, can be seen. There is also an abundance of marram grass, which has helped to preserve the area over the years. In the 14th century a series of violent storms buried a large part of the sand dunes. The residents feared that the dunes would be completed swallowed and the town prompted Queen Elizabeth I to bring in a law that would protect the marram grass, the roots of which helped to stabilise the dunes. This stopped the advance of the dunes and also provided the raw material for a new industry, the weaving of marram grass leaves to form mats. With nothing to restrict them, rabbits soon colonised the dunes, giving the area the name of Newborough Warren. This provided the residents with another valuable natural resource and, during its heyday, one hundred thousand rabbits a year were taken from the warren. However the outbreak of myxomytosis in the 1950's reduced the rabbit population and allowed the vegetation to spread once more.

We have already discovered that Ynys Môn is a progressive, futuristic island, and has learned to cope and grow with its environment. It can claim to be the first to try out many new concepts, for example, the first branch of the Woman's institute was formed on the island in 1915, and in September 1949, the first comprehensive school in England and Wales was opened at Caergybi (Holyhead). Ynys Môn was, in 1955, the first place in Britain to have a fluoridated water supply, and in 1972, the second nuclear power station came into service.

Wylfa Nuclear Power Station on the A5025 near Cemaes on the north side of Anglesey, generates enough electricity to serve two cities the size of Liverpool. The station has many 'hands-on' displays, a multi-media show and a guided tour every day. There is an interesting tale attached to the construction of the station. Whilst excavating a tunnel the workmen kept seeing the ghostly figure of a woman who was dressed in white and hummed songs as she glided between them. After several visits, some of the workmen became frightened, gave up their jobs, and moved away. Apparently, it was later discovered that an opera singer, Rosina Buckman, once lived in a house, called Galan Ddu, and it is claimed that the box containing her ashes was disturbed during the excavations.

From the power of electricity, perhaps we should think about the power of wind and its ability to generate electricity cleanly. There are a number of wind farms in Wales but the most impressive is on Ynys Môn. Thus proving, yet again, that the island can adapt and move with the ever changing market-place.

From the air power, we move to those who wished to be airborne. A very few of the elderly residents can still recall the day when aviation arrived on the island. It was on Wednesday, 10 August 1910, that the first aircraft appeared over the north-western part of the island. It had been an extremely hot day and by 7.00pm the worst of the heat was over. Suddenly there appeared in the sky a Farina biplane, piloted by Robert Lorraine, a larger than life aviation pioneer. During that week he had taken part in a flying meeting at Blackpool, and was making plans to fly from Holyhead to Dublin and in so doing become the first airman to cross the Irish Sea. His friend, George Smart made the necessary arrangements and, thanks to the good weather, Robert set off from Blackpool at about 6.30am, with the intention of flying along the North Wales coast until he reached Holyhead. Following in a car, which was another modern invention at the time, was his mechanic Jules Vedrines and his brother Emil.

The flight did not go well because Emil had not set the controls correctly, putting an enormous strain on the control cables. Lorraine was forced to land at Llandrillo-yn-Rhos, and in doing so, became the first man to land in North Wales!

The Vedrines brothers took the rest of the day to re-set the plane and it was 5pm in the evening before Robert was ready for take off again. He had planned to use the railway lines as his guide but, for some reason, decided to follow the Anglesey Coast and, due to the heat haze, became completely lost. Soon he found himself wandering aimlessly further out to sea, with a rapidly emptying fuel tank. Disaster was imminent, so he decided to use the sun's position to guide him back to Ynys Môn. Just one mile from the shore the engine cut out and he glided earthwards, filled with fear. To his relief, he touched down in a field and was immediately surrounded by a group of curious children.

The following day George Smart looked at the area, threw his hands up in the air, and declared that it was a 'strip of wilderness'. The short journey to Holyhead was considered unsafe because of the high wind but after two days, it had died down sufficiently. With the help of some of the villagers, the aircraft was taken to the top of a slope so that the downhill run would help the plane to become airborne. The runway was clear, except for a mound of about fifteen feet (four and a half metres), which Robert hoped he could clear on his take-off run. Unfortunately he failed and the plane crashed into the mound, causing serious damage. A temporary hanger was hurriedly rigged up by the farmer on whose land the plane was landbound, and work to repair the damage began in earnest.

Meanwhile Robert Lorraine, who was a successful actor-manager and close friend of George Bernard Shaw, who it appears treated him like a son, returned to London. The farmer, being of enterprising Môn stock lost no time in making some money out of the disaster. He set up a table and starting selling refreshments to the visitors who came to see the biplane. There is no doubt that profit was his aim, as his prices show. A glass of water cost 3d and a glass of milk a shilling. He also claimed fifty-six pounds from Robert Lorraine, for damage caused to the farm by the many visitors.

On September 4, the aircraft had been repaired and Lorraine was back in Ynys Môn ready for the forthcoming flight. It was a perfect day, a light gentle wind glided over the island, but no one had noticed that the field chosen for take-off was a reclaimed bog. The engine was started up and the plane slowly began its take-off, but then suddenly came to a halt, after only a few yards. It shuddered and jerked forward, the wheels and centre section collapsed and pinned Robert by his legs in the cock-pit. Luckily he suffered no more than bruised limbs and dented pride. By now he had had enough, and was on the verge of giving up, when his friend Smart persuaded him to make one last attempt. The plane, now a sorry heap of splintered wood and torn fabric, was carefully loaded onto a farm-cart and taken to Holyhead. Lorraine's acting commitments demanded him to be back in London within a week, so the Verdines brothers set to work immediately.

On September 11, he finally became airborne and left Holyhead to embark on an exciting record-breaking flight. Sadly, it was not to be. Lorraine almost reached the Irish coast, but just failed to reach land.

After this Lorraine abandoned aviation for good, whilst his mechanic Jules Verdines went on to become one of France's leading pilots. He survived the First World War but was killed in a flying accident in 1919. However, the first Irish sea crossing was finally achieved by Vivian Hewitt, a Rhyl aviator in April 1912. Although the sight of a plane in the air over Ynys Môn was a novel experience then, today it is common place, with the Royal Air Force base at Valley which was established in 1941 as a World War Two fighter base. In 1943 the United States Air Force took over and developed the airfield into a major Trans-Atlantic terminal for thousands of US airmen. To many United States airmen Valley was their first sight of Europe. After the war the Royal Air Force resumed responsibility for the base and today it is the only advanced jet flying school in the RAF. It is open at all times to receive aircraft in difficulty and also has a Marine Craft Unit, an Air-Sea Rescue Service, as well as a Strike Command Missile Practice Camp. The name Valley does not appear to have been mentioned before 1822, and it is thought that it was a literal description used by Thomas Telford, during the construction of the A5 when creating a cutting through the small local hill.

If you are a resident of, or if your visit to, Ynys Môn includes a trip 'down memory lane' then The Museum of Childhood at Beaumaris is the place for you. The museum was the Islands oldest independent attraction from 1973 to 1994 and has thousands of exhibits in its nine rooms which cater for all ages and fascinations. The highlights are a hoard of dolls, trains sets and piggy banks, as well as a stereoscopic viewer designed in 1850 to show some of the earliest 3D moving images.

If the world of make believe and little people is your forte, then Anglesey's Model Village at Niwbwrch (Newborough) is a place where you can view the island's historical landmarks in miniature. You can meander through the pleasant one acre landscaped gardens, or take a ride on the working model garden railway which makes a regular stop at the village of Llanfairpwllgwyngyllgogerychwyrndrobwllllantysiliogogogoch.

Brynsiencyn, once a Druid centre, is now home to the imaginative Anglesey Sea Zoo. Here the visitor can see hundreds of strange and beautiful marine inhabitants in their natural environment, and watch baby seahorses and conger eels swim in and out of an old shipwreck. At Pili-Palas north of Porthaethwy (Menai Bridge) it is the world of butterflies, birds and creepy crawlies that takes its turn in exciting the visitor. Beware also of Cedric the Snake!

Since 1993 Sealynx Catamarans, introduced by Stena Sealink, have run from Holyhead to Dun Laoghaire, six miles south of Dublin, in just two hours. The latest sailing can be checked with Stena Sealink ferries and many visitors to the Isle of Anglesey take advantage of a trip which can cost as little as £8, although this does entail catching a 4a.m. ferry. However the Sealynx day trips can be more convenient and shorter, but twice as expensive.

I do hope that having read the book and explored some of the lesser known areas of Ynys Môn you will return to the island, because one visit, like one book, is not enough to encapsulate the essence of the area. Perhaps you too will fall in love with this part of Ancient Wales and learn to enjoy what it has to offer.

Bibliography

Various volumes of Transactions by Anglesey Antiquarian Society and Field Club

Various issues of Country Quest magazine from 1970-1999

Prehistoric Anglesey by Frances Lynch (Second edition), published by Anglesey Antiquarian Society, 1991

Medieval Anglesey by A.D. Carr, published by Anglesey Antiquarian Society Llangefni, 1982

Welsh Folklore, a collection of the folklore tales and legends of North Wales – Elias Owen, published by Llanerch, 1996

Wales Through the Ages Vol 1 and 2, edited by A.J. Roderick, published by Christopher Davies Ltd., 1965

The Rivers of Anglesey by Gwilym T. Jones, published by Research Centre of Wales University College of North Wales Bangor, 1989

Wales and Archaeological Guide – the prehistoric, Roman and early Medieval Field Monuments by Christopher Houlder, published by Faber and Faber

Anglesey and North West Coast by Francis Henry Glazebrook, published by Bookland & Co. Ltd., Bangor

The Companion Guide to North Wales by Elisabeth Beazley and Peter Howell, published by Collins, 1975

The Queen's Wales – North Wales by H.L.V. Fletcher, published by Hodder and Stoughton

Historic Places of Wales by W.T. Barber by Moorland Publishing

The Shell Guide to Wales by Wynford Vaughan-Thomas and Alun Llewellyn

A History of Wales by John Davies, published by Penguin

The Dictionary of Welsh Biography down to 1940 – under the auspices of The Honourable Society of Cymmrodorion, published London, 1959

INDEX

Full catalogue and price list available from:
GWASG CARREG GWALCH,
12 Iard yr Orsaf, Llanrwst, Conwy, Wales, LL26 0EH.